921 - Sn   JUL   '68

Winehouse

The Duke Snider story

DATE DUE			
SEP 27 '68			
NOV 29 7			
DEC 4			
DEC 2			
DEC 1 7			
FEB 18			
MAR 1 1			
DEC 2			
DEC 1 7			
APR 20			

THE DUKE SNIDER STORY

"He has steel springs in his legs and dynamite in his bat." That was part of a glowing scouting report sent to the Brooklyn Dodgers about a husky high school athlete named Edwin Donald Snider. Although Branch Rickey signed the seventeen-year-old sensation, he never dreamed that the young Californian would reign for more than a decade as the illustrious "Duke of Flatbush" and that his explosive bat would help bring the Dodgers seven National League pennants and two world championships.

PeeWee Reese, Marv Rackley, Duke Snider, Jackie
Robinson (1948).

The Dodger center fielder takes
a tumble as he tries for ball hit
by Stan Musial of the Cardinals.

Snider makes spectacular leap
to rob Yankee Joe Collins of an
extra base hit in 1953 Series.

Snider shows his speed on the basepaths, scoring
all the way from first on Robinson's single (1950).

Dodgers' hustling center fielder
"climbs" Ebbets Field outfield wall in
game with the Giants (1954).

The Duke connects for a homer in
sixth game of 1959 World Series.

Duke Snider Night, August 27, 1960. With him are his wife Beverly and their children.

Duke made his TV acting debut in 1959 on "The Rifleman" with Chuck Connors, ex-Dodger teammate.

All former Dodgers — Holmes, Furillo, Hodges, Newcombe, Abrams and Branca surround Campanella and Snider (1963).

Snider receives the Catholic Youth Organization of New York's annual "Most Popular Met Player" Award on August 8, 1963.

Gil Hodges and Duke Snider, both former Dodgers, now with the New York Mets (1963).

Duke Snider keeps in physical shape by working on his 60-acre ranch at Fallbrook, California (1957).

THE **DUKE SNIDER** STORY

by Irwin Winehouse

 Julian Messner   **New York**

Published by Julian Messner
Division of Pocket Books, Inc.
8 West 40th Street, New York 10018

© Copyright 1964 by Irwin Winehouse

Third Printing, 1965

Photographs used with the permission of
Wide World Photos and United Press International

Printed in the United States of America

Library of Congress Catalog Card No. 64–11367

For my team:

ARTHUR, BRENT, BRYAN, CARL, GAVIN,
GLENN, JEFFREY, RICHARD AND STEPHEN

THE DUKE SNIDER STORY

1

●●●●●●●●●●●●●●●●●●●●●●●●●●●●●●●

"Here he comes!" Ward Snider announced proudly.

"Is he all right?" Florence Snider joined her husband at the front window and gazed anxiously down the street.

"When are you going to stop worrying?" he chided her gently. "He's a big boy now."

"He's only a baby. This is his first day of school."

Ward Snider grinned. "Look at the cocky walk. Steps out as if he was ready to lick the world."

"The world's more likely to lick him," Mrs. Snider said with anxiety still in her voice. She remembered her son's long history of illness—chicken pox at three months which settled in his eyelids and threatened his vision until an old Japanese doctor cured it; mumps; two attacks of measles.

"For goodness sake, Flo!" Ward Snider protested.

"That boy's got good German-Dutch blood on my side, and Scotch-Irish on yours. That's the best of the best!" He stepped to the door and flung it open.

A handsome, blue-eyed, five-year-old came striding into the house.

"Here comes His Majesty, the Duke!" Mr. Snider lifted his son high into the air and swung him around the room. His wife smiled, caught up by the infectious warmth and hopes of her husband for their boy.

As Edwin Donald Snider sailed about the room in his father's arms, there was a feeling of fun, joy and confidence. He had two loving parents; he had come through his first day at kindergarten with flying colors, and he had received a nickname which would stay with him for the rest of his life—"Duke."

Ward Snider was an ex-Navy man whose motto was: "Play hard and work hard. Makes you live longer and laugh louder." After a hitch as a chief boatswain's mate, he had married a shy, pretty, Coffeyville, Kansas, girl and brought her to the West Coast. When he wasn't playing semipro ball, Ward Snider worked as a rigger in the Southern California shipyards.

He and his bride had moved to a tiny cottage on the outskirts of Whittier, California, and there, on September 19, 1926, Edwin Donald Snider was born.

Florence Snider sat up nights with her sickly son, nursed him through one childhood illness after another and worried because Edwin—she never called him Duke —was a nervous child.

But Ward Snider wasn't the type to pamper any boy

[10]

of his. Now that Duke was old enough to attend school, he was old enough to "play ball."

"Pop, it feels funny this way," Duke complained.

"You'll get used to it."

The towheaded youngster stood in a corner of the school playground, at the left side of an improvised plate, clutching his first dime-store bat.

"Let me try it from the other side." Duke crossed to the opposite side of the plate and switched the grip on his bat.

"Get back where I told you!" his father roared. He yanked at his cap and came storming in from the mound.

"But Pop . . ."

"No buts about it! You learn to bat left-handed. That way you'll always be two steps closer to first base."

Ward Snider took his baseball seriously. He was determined to pass along every trick he knew to his son. By the end of the day Duke was swinging from the left side of the plate as if it was the most natural thing in the world.

After the workout, as the pair headed for home, Ward Snider launched into the first of his many "lectures" on batting strategy.

"When you stand at the plate, you've got to be comfortable. Keep your head and eyes toward the pitcher; your hands and elbows away from your body." He stopped to emphasize a point. "You've got to be in balance. At ease. But most important, keep your front shoulder pointed toward the pitcher until the last second

[11]

before you swing. That way you can hit curve balls and outside pitches."

Ward Snider was not an easy taskmaster, and Duke listened attentively to everything he said. Discussing those formative days Mr. Snider once told a reporter: "I insisted he play the game right, from the start. It wasn't always easy. Once I had to whack his butt. But it helped cure him of backing up on fly balls and ground balls, which gives the runner an advantage."

When Ward Snider tried his son at pitching, he discovered that the six-year-old Duke had an unusually strong arm. Since a pitcher has to have a proper target, Mrs. Snider was brought along next day. And there, in the school playground, while his father served as catcher and his mother stood at the plate, bat in hand, Duke fired pitch after pitch. With daily practice, he could soon throw a fast one high or low and break off a curve.

The practice sessions continued for six months; then Ward Snider decided his son was ready for a trial-by-fire. As they turned into the playground, he spotted a group of twelve- and thirteen-year-olds about to choose up sides for a game.

"Go on over and tell them you want to play," he said as he pushed his son forward.

"They won't let me, Pop. I'm too young."

"You don't know 'til you ask." Ward Snider's voice hardened. "Go ahead."

Duke started toward the cluster of boys, then stopped and turned back. "Pa . . ."

"You want me to take you to Wrigley Field to meet Jigger Statz, don't you?"

Duke nodded. The stylish ex-Brooklyn outfielder was playing for Los Angeles of the Pacific Coast League, and the youngster wanted desperately to meet him.

"Okay, then," Mr. Snider said, pointing to the group of young ballplayers. "Get going!"

As Duke walked up, one of the boys asked, "What do you want, kid?"

"I'd like to play."

"Go on home."

"I can pitch," Duke persisted.

"Who says?"

"Me."

There was a round of laughter. "Come on," one of the bigger boys announced. "Let's get this game under way." To Duke he added derisively, "Go play hopscotch and stop bothering us."

Duke stood his ground. He knew his father was watching, and he would get no sympathy if he turned and ran. Fighting back his fears, he held up the bat in his hand. "I'll bet this bat I can strike you out!"

Suddenly there was silence; the group had heard the challenge. Now all eyes turned toward the skinny six-year-old. "Take him up on it, Charlie," one of the players shouted. "We can always use an extra bat."

The boy called Charlie, apparently the team's best batter, stepped confidently up to the plate. "It'll be like stealing candy from a baby." He took a few vicious cuts at the air, then glanced toward Duke. "Well? What're you waiting for? Let's see what makes you so good!"

Duke picked up the ball and started out to the mound. He tried to remember everything he had been told, but now it all seemed a jumble. In a moment, everybody would be laughing at him, and he would have lost his new bat to boot. How would he explain *that* to his father? As he stepped onto the rubber, one phrase his father repeated constantly leaped out from the maze of strategy and advice he had been given: "Relax, boy! Just learn to relax."

Duke dropped his hands to his side and took two deep breaths. As he exhaled, he felt the tension fall away. Placing his fingers across the seams of the ball, he went into his motion and zipped the ball toward the plate. The batter swung and missed. It was a fast ball, low and inside.

"Come on! Come on!" Charlie shouted. "Get it over the plate."

Duke sent the next one down the middle, but Charlie had no better luck the second time. Now his teammates got on his back.

"What's the matter!" one of them called. "The kid got you dizzy?"

"This one goes over the fence," Charlie announced confidently as he held his bat in readiness. "Just watch and see."

About to pitch for the third time, Duke remembered something else his father had said: "Take a little extra time once in a while. It keeps the batter on edge. Throws off his timing."

Duke brushed some imaginary dust from his sleeve, then slowly straightened his cap. This time he double-pumped before delivering.

The overanxious batter swung long before the ball reached the plate. Duke Snider had his first strike-out.

The players shouted their approval as they clustered around, asking Duke to pitch in their game.

"Maybe tomorrow," he said, picking up his bat and walking off. "My Pop's taking me to Wrigley Field today to meet Jigger Statz."

From then on, Duke played regularly with boys twice his age and soon developed into the sensation of the neighborhood. But, he had one failing.

He played as if his life depended upon it, always trying to prove he was good—prove it to his father; prove it to his teammates; prove it to himself. After each game, he replayed in his mind every inning, relived every pitch, and was plagued by each error.

By the time he was twelve, Duke began at last to look his age. In two years he had grown seven and a half inches. At fifteen, he stood almost six feet tall and weighed 150 pounds.

The family moved from Whittier to nearby Compton, and at Enterprise Junior High School, under coach Ralph Rozelle, Duke became an outstanding pitcher. Though he preferred to play the outfield, Rozelle kept him on the mound. But when he played "Sunday Ball"— semipro ball—with a local team called the Compton

Merchants, Duke held down the position he liked best, center field.

The local newspapers began to refer to him as "a natural athlete, a kid with talent who should go far."

Each morning before classes began, Coach Rozelle put his team through a short, practice session. One day Duke came to bat with the score tied, 2–2, and promptly slapped a base hit into right field. A teammate followed with a line-drive slice over third.

With the hit-and-run on, Duke decided to go for all the marbles. He raced past second and headed for third. The outfielder got his hands on the ball as Duke rounded third and began to dig for home with the tie-breaking run.

"Slide, Duke! Slide!" his teammates urged.

It would be a close call at the plate. Duke set himself to slide, then suddenly remembered the new school clothes he was wearing. He shifted his weight and continued to charge the plate. Then, without sliding, he touched home plate with his left leg and tried to stop at the same time. The sudden motion wrenched his left leg, twisting the cartilage in his knee.

It all happened so quickly, Duke didn't feel the pain until he tried to get to his feet. Then he sank to the ground again.

"What the devil are you trying to do?" Ralph Rozelle shouted.

"Didn't want to mess up my good clothes."

"Then don't play ball without changing," Rozelle snapped angrily.

"I'm sorry," Duke replied sheepishly.

"You ought to be! Pulling a boneheaded stunt like that!" Rozelle lifted his star performer to his feet and helped him off the field. "You'll get your share of bumps and bangs," he said not unkindly. "Don't go looking to manufacture any."

Four days later, the pain had disappeared and the injury was forgotten. Duke went back to winning new laurels on the mound and dreamed of becoming a major leaguer. But, as it did with so many other families, December 7, 1941, changed the plans of the Snider family and their fifteen-year-old son.

Duke knew there was something wrong the moment he entered the house and saw his father's face.

"What's the matter, Pop?" he asked, anxiety creeping into his voice.

"New job," came the response, but Duke sensed all was not well. His father glanced across the kitchen at his mother, busy at the stove. Slowly she turned and Duke could see she had been crying.

"What's going on?" he demanded. "Will somebody *please* answer me?"

"Your father has been called back into the Navy."

They had all been expecting it, yet when it came, it was like a blow between the eyes. Duke crossed to the table and sat down. His mother poured him a glass of milk but he didn't touch it.

"Chief petty officer," his father added. "Been assigned to a PT boat in the Pacific."

Duke kept his eyes on the glass of milk. Suddenly he

thought: Milk is for kids. Got problems now, new responsibilities. Have to act like a man. "Don't worry, Pop," he said. "I'll help out."

"You just keep going to school!" his mother said.

"I want to help."

"You do as your Mom says. She knows best." There was none of the usual lightheartedness in his father's voice.

"We'll manage," Mrs. Snider said. "I've been promised a defense job at a plastics plant."

"I can still help," Duke persisted.

"You just get good grades," his mother said. "That's all the help I need."

Duke looked searchingly at his father. How long would he be away? Would he *ever* come back?

He fought back the tears as his mother placed a slice of pie before the still-untouched glass of milk.

"Go on, have your milk," she said. "Your father will have this war finished off singlehanded in six months!"

Duke could see the tears in her eyes as she turned back to the stove. One thing he knew for sure: he wouldn't let his mother carry the burden alone. He had to help but he knew his part-time job delivering papers wouldn't be enough. Then, suddenly, he knew exactly what he would do.

"Hey, kid! Where you going? The game doesn't start for an hour."

"I want to see the manager."

"You got an appointment?"

Duke had made up his mind to take a crack at the big time. He had hitched a ride into Los Angeles, and now stood at the entrance to Wrigley Field, the home of the Angels. If he was as good as they said, he was good enough to play major league ball. Then he could really help his mother pay the bills.

"You got an appointment?" the gatekeeper repeated.

"No," Duke admitted, then added hopefully, "but I know Jigger Statz."

The white-haired man smiled. "Jigger's been gone for years. What do you want, a job selling peanuts and popcorn?"

"I want to try out for the team."

"Haven't you heard?" the gateman declared dryly. "We're full up."

"Please, mister, get me in to see the manager."

"Kid, go on home. You're wasting your time."

Duke thought of pushing past the man and rushing through the gate. Instead he said: "All I want is a trial."

The old man took out a handkerchief and mopped his brow. "Look, kid," he said sympathetically, "I've seen hundreds like you. They all think they can play major league ball. It's part of growing up. Like every girl wants to be a movie star."

"I'm good!" Duke blurted out.

The man laughed. "Sure. With a bunch of kids your own age."

Duke felt the anger welling up inside him. "I asked to see the manager. I didn't come here for a lecture."

"Don't get steamed up," the gatekeeper said not unkindly. "I got a grandson your age or I wouldn't be wasting all this time."

Duke tried to keep himself under control. If he didn't get past the gateman and into the park, the whole trip would have been for nothing. He remembered the first time he wanted to get into a game and they wouldn't let him. He had waved a bat and bravely announced: "I'll bet this bat I can strike you out!" But now it wasn't that simple. All he could do was beg.

"Please, mister, just call and ask."

"Who said you're so good?" the man wanted to know. "Your father?"

"That's right," Duke admitted, then added proudly, "He's in the Navy. Fighting in the Pacific."

"Oh," the gatekeeper said, weakening. "Why didn't you say your Pop was in the Navy. Served myself in the first World War." He stepped into his booth and picked up the phone.

Duke couldn't hear the conversation, but at one point, the man poked his head out to ask: "How old are you?"

"Fifteen," Duke said, then added, "and a half."

The gateman relayed the vital statistic. A few seconds later he hung up the phone and turned towards Duke shaking his head. "Too young. Boss says come back in about two years."

"But I need a chance now!"

"Look, son," the gatekeeper said gently, "if you're good now, you'll be that much better in two years."

"I thought there was a shortage of players," Duke persisted. "Everybody going off to the war."

"I guess they just haven't gotten down to the fifteen-year-olds yet. Come on," the man said as he opened the gate. "I'll let you in to see the game for free."

"No thanks," Duke replied gently. "I've got to get back to my newspaper route."

"Don't forget. Two years."

"I won't," Duke said, then turned and walked slowly away.

2

Duke returned from that afternoon at Wrigley Field more determined than ever to prove he was pro material. At Compton High School he was a member of the baseball, basketball, and football squads. Coach Bill Schleibaum encouraged him to continue in all three, but warned him not to drive himself.

"I only know one way to play," Duke said, "and that's to win."

"Right," Schleibaum agreed, "but don't let it take all the fun out of sports."

Duke tried, but for him "the game" was no longer play. It had become a means toward an end, a way of life to bring security and success—things he could share with his family.

In his junior year, Duke played the outfield for most

of the season until Coach Schleibaum needed him on the mound. Then he came in to finish one game and went on to win the next eight straight!

With the fall, Duke put on his maroon and gray jersey with the number eleven on it and overwhelmed the opposition as Compton's star quarterback. On Armistice Day, against the highly favored Woodrow Wilson Bruins, he completed ten out of eighteen passes for three touchdowns, while compiling over 220 yards in completions and running.

"Relying on the cool, confident, calculating, powerful, accurate arm of Duke Snider," an enthusiastic sports reporter stated, "the Tarbabes passed their way to an 18–13 victory and virtually assured themselves of the Long Beach–Compton championship."

In a game against Long Beach Poly, Duke caught the attention of Coach Jimmy Phelan from St. Mary's College.

The game was a thriller right down to the wire. With forty seconds left to play, and Compton behind 19–13, Duke faded back as his pass receiver streaked down the field. This one had to count. He waited until the last possible moment, then threw. The ball sailed sixty-three yards straight to its target. The touchdown pass and extra point put Compton High over the top, 20–19.

As he watched, Jim Phelan knew he was seeing one of the finest ball handlers in the state. Two weeks later in the league championship game against Jordan High School, Duke did even better. He heaved a touchdown pass that carried sixty-eight yards in the air. Though

Compton lost the championship, Jim Phelan made up his mind. He wanted Duke Snider for St. Mary's College.

"Mom, it doesn't make sense," Duke insisted.

"At least you'll have an education," Mrs. Snider replied.

"I'm a ballplayer. I'm not a student. I don't want to be an engineer or a doctor or a lawyer."

"Mr. Phelan says . . ."

Suddenly Duke understood his mother's interest in the rewards of higher education. Jim Phelan had talked to him about a football scholarship. Evidently, his mother had been exposed to the same arguments. "Mom," Duke began and his voice was all seriousness, "God gave me something special. I'm not letting it go to waste while I spend four years at some college studying physical education."

"You'll still be able to play ball."

"And wait four years before I can become a pro and earn a living?"

Mrs. Snider turned away. She wished Ward were here to back her up. But even if he were, he would probably have sided with his son. "Have you talked it over with Bev?" she asked, referring to Duke's pretty brown-eyed girl friend, Beverly Null.

Duke's lips tightened with annoyance. "All you women think alike!" he announced. It was apparent he had received little support from Beverly.

"Son," Florence Snider said as she placed a hand on Duke's shoulder, "why not give it a little more thought?

[24]

You won't always have a chance for an education. Think of it as insurance. Something to have—just in case."

"Mom," Duke said with a playful chuckle, "I guess you just don't know how good I really am."

Duke's outstanding skill in football and baseball was equaled in basketball. He was called "the coolest player seen on the Compton hardwoods for quite a spell." His forte was an ability to hit the bucket from any angle. Duke's scoring total that season was 175 points, which helped win him the Helms Athletic Foundation Award. He made all-section or all–Southern California in three sports, and managed to maintain a B-plus average.

In the spring of his senior year, Duke was back on the mound for the Tarbabes. The most eagerly anticipated game was the annual battle against Beverly Hills High.

On the mound for Compton was the handsome, blue-eyed six-footer who had held the Beverly Hills team hitless for six innings. Now, as Duke stepped to the mound to face the first batter in the top of the seventh, he could sense something strange in the air. Why had the fans suddenly grown quiet and tense? The six previous innings had been an effortless performance. Everything went right. His control never faltered. Duke picked up the rosin bag, squeezed it in his hand, then dropped it to his side. As he glanced toward the catcher for his signal, he heard a fan shout encouragingly: "Come on, Duke! You've got a no-hitter going!"

Duke swept through the seventh and eighth. Finally he faced the last three batters in the ninth inning. The first man popped up. Duke struck the second man out. As the ball was whipped around the infield, Duke glanced toward the dugout. Seated beside Bill Schleibaum was a man he recognized as Pat Patterson, a scout for the Cincinnati Reds. The sight of Patterson momentarily shook Duke. He walked the next batter.

Schleibaum was on his feet. "Finish this one off, Duke! It's getting late and my wife has dinner on the stove!"

Duke smiled. The coach always grew hungry when the pressure mounted. Duke fired one down the middle for a strike. The batter fouled the next pitch. And on a change-of-pace, Duke got his man out swinging. He had pitched a no-hitter!

With a shout of victory, Duke's teammates lifted their beaming hero onto their shoulders and began to parade him around the diamond. It was the happiest day in Duke Snider's young life.

The stadium was in an uproar. Schleibaum let out a howl and pounded Patterson on the back. "*Now* what do you say? Is my boy good enough for Cincinnati?"

In the course of the 7–0 no-hitter, Duke had collected four hits in five trips to the plate.

"He's good enough," the Cincinnati scout admitted. "Just don't go stuffing his head with fancy notions about what he's worth."

Schleibaum beamed as Patterson walked off. It wasn't every day he found a great star.

"Why hasn't he come to see me?" Duke demanded sullenly.

Schleibaum shook his head, and took another bite of hamburger. The coach and his star were seated in the local diner discussing Snider's future. There had been no action from Pat Patterson. The Reds' scout had studied Duke at the high school, watched him play .400 ball with the Compton Merchants, but still no offer. Duke had graduated from high school at the end of the winter term, and the waiting was beginning to tell.

"Doesn't he think I'm good enough?"

"I don't know," Schleibaum admitted. "After that no-hitter last September I figured you were in."

"That was six months ago!"

Schleibaum shook his head again. "I'd have bet money Patterson was ready to offer you a bonus to sign."

Duke stared at the Coke before him. He had made so many plans, been so sure of himself. Now, the grinding doubt began to set in. He had said no to Phelan and had convinced his mother and Beverly he would make a pro team this year. Sure he was only seventeen and a half—but that was old enough. The war had really crippled most clubs, and if he couldn't make it now, he never would. All he had expected from Patterson was $2,500 for signing. Just enough to let his mother pay off the mortgage on the house. But it hadn't happened. Not even a hint of an offer.

"Duke," Schleibaum warned, "don't press. It'll come."

"I wish I were sure." Duke tried to fight back the frustration, but when he felt unhappy, it showed. He got to his feet. "Thanks for the Coke, Coach."

"Forget it. Next time we'll be celebrating with champagne. You wait and see."

Duke forced a smile. "I'll keep telling myself that." And then, he headed toward the door.

A stranger stepped up to the Snider house on 138th Street in Compton and pressed the bell.

Duke answered the door. He saw a short, stocky man in a business suit and mistook him for a door-to-door salesman.

"Sorry, but my mother's at work."

"That's all right, Duke," the man said. "I came to talk to you."

"What about?" Duke asked cautiously.

"The Brooklyn Dodgers. I'm Tom Downey."

Duke had heard of the Brooklyn scout.

"Hi!" he said. "Come on in."

"I've come to sign you," Downey said as he dropped his heavy frame into the big overstuffed chair in the Snider living room.

"Gosh, Mr. Downey," Duke stammered, "I don't know what to say."

"You want to play for Brooklyn, don't you?"

Relax. Relax, Duke told himself. Don't be too eager. You're pulling for big stakes. Play him off against Patterson.

"Mr. Patterson has been around," Duke began.

Downey nodded. "I know. And he hasn't made you an offer."

"He will!" Duke tried his best to sound convincing.

"Sorry, son, but he won't. You're too young. Cincinnati hasn't the time to wait. They need manpower now. You can forget about Patterson."

The blood drained from Duke's face. He couldn't be worth much to the Dodgers if the Reds didn't want him.

"We operate a little differently," the Brooklyn scout explained. "We know you're not ready, but we can afford to wait. Mr. Rickey," Downey was referring to Branch Rickey, the Dodger president, "is out to build a farm system that will beat the one he set up for the Cardinals. To us, you're a good prospect."

"But I'm ready for the majors," Duke said hopefully.

Downey shook his head. "You're ready—to start learning."

Duke wanted to convince the chunky little man he wasn't just a good amateur. "I was offered a college scholarship . . ."

"Kid," Downey interjected, "you don't have to prove how good you are to me. If I didn't believe you had it, I wouldn't be here."

Duke wondered if he sounded ungrateful. He didn't mean to. It was just the hurt of knowing Patterson didn't want him. Sure he'd grab at the chance to be with the Dodgers, but he hated not to have a choice.

"We'll give you seven hundred fifty to sign."

And that was the deal. The long-anticipated $2,500 bonus had shrunk to a meager $750. It was as if Downey had said: "You may be big league in Compton, but you're only a question mark in Brooklyn."

[29]

"I'll have to write to my father. He's serving in the Pacific." The disappointment in Duke's voice was obvious.

"You do that," Downey said, getting to his feet, "and let me know."

3

●●●●●●●●●●●●●●●●●●●●●●●●●●●●●●●●●●●●

"Edwin, be careful."

"Don't worry, Mom."

They were at Union Station in downtown Los Angeles. Duke was about to board the Union Pacific for Chicago and then on to the East Coast.

"You have your ticket?" the worried Mrs. Snider asked.

Duke nodded. Tom Downey had given him a ticket to the Dodger's wartime training camp at Bear Mountain, New York. "You'll travel east with Hal Gregg, one of our pitchers," Downey had advised. "And get some warm clothes. There's still snow up there."

Duke had never seen snow, or traveled across the United States, and he could scarcely wait for the trip to begin. He also wanted to talk baseball with Hal Gregg, and get the real low-down on what to expect.

"Don't forget to write," Duke said to Beverly who was standing shyly off to one side.

She smiled and dropped her eyes. "I'll remember."

" 'Board!" came the conductor's call. Duke grabbed his suitcase, kissed his mother, gave Beverly a peck on the cheek, and swung up onto the train.

The trip east was a panorama of a million new impressions as Duke sat beside the window gazing out across the varied landscape. But, uppermost in his mind were the things Gregg had told him about the Dodger system.

Early in 1943, Dodger president Branch Rickey had instituted his youth program in a search for raw talent with which to rebuild the Dodgers once the war was over. He wanted youth, the younger the better, since there was less likelihood that such prospects would be drafted.

Special letters were sent to some 18,000 high school baseball coaches, and more than 4,000 had sent Rickey their prime recommendations. Bill Schleibaum had recommended Duke Snider. The Dodger president and his staff had cut the number down to 2,000, and at temporary try-out camps all over the country, Dodger scouts had inspected the boys in wholesale lots. Four hundred had been signed. One of the 400 was Duke Snider.

Tom Downey had seen enough of Duke to preclude a trip to a tryout camp. But at best, Duke now considered himself only an insignificant rookie who would be tossed out into the farm system along with 399 other green apples to see how they would ripen.

"You either got it or you haven't," Gregg said.

"I've got it!" Duke maintained.

"Great. But look at it this way," Gregg suggested philosophically. "Maybe you waste a year or two. If it doesn't work out, you had your kicks. You're still young. You can always sell insurance or marry a rich girl."

Duke couldn't take his career that lightly. Time was all he had. Just so many good years—and he wasn't about to waste them. He *had* to make good!

The best advice Gregg could give was: "Get in there, hustle, and hope they don't send you down to Jake Pitler's 'day nursery' at Newport News."

The train rolled on, passed the wind-swept prairies and the cities, the parched deserts and the winding rivers, the valleys and the snow-topped mountains, moving Duke Snider ever closer to that distant Bear Mountain camp and the promise it held.

Up the Hudson River some fifty miles north of New York City and Ebbets Field lay the mountain resort area which the Dodgers were using as a wartime expedient in 1944.

Cold and hungry, Duke climbed down from the bus he and Gregg had boarded in New York, and soon found himself herded into a noisy barracks building filled with a dozen other rookies. Most of them, he noticed, were fifteen- and sixteen-year-olds. Duke felt better. They looked more like a bunch of Boy Scouts than major league prospects. Confidently, he walked across the bare wooden floor and dropped his suitcase beside an empty cot. He had stopped worrying about the competition.

Duke received his first jolt when rookie coach Wid

Matthews laid down the law in his official welcome. It was brief, to the point, and far from Boy Scout talk: "We expect you to get out there and work. Show us what you've got. Follow orders and keep your mouth shut."

Duke couldn't wait to show Wid Matthews what he could do. Even more important, he wanted to catch the eye of both Dodger manager Leo Durocher and Branch Rickey, Jr. The latter was helping his father lay the groundwork for the Brooklyn postwar farm system. But, instead of playing ball, Duke along with the other rookies was doing calisthenics.

When the exercise sessions were over, he found himself running around the sixty-yard cinder path in full baseball uniform. In his second try, he was clocked at a very respectable 6.7 seconds. (At that time, the world's record for a man in a track suit was 6.1.)

Next, Duke and a half-dozen aspiring outfielders were placed on a throwing line 400 feet from home plate and ordered to whip the ball in. With his amazing arm, Duke produced his famous "clothesline" throw that traveled in a low trajectory to the plate without a bounce and landed in the strike zone. Once was not enough to prove the point. He was made to repeat the performance until he wound up with a sore arm. To an eager, seventeen-year-old competitor it all seemed a great waste of time.

Then, on the third day, Wid Matthews spotted Duke sitting down when he should have been doing field laps. A straightforward, no-nonsense type, he lowered the boom with a bang: "Turn in your uniform and get out!"

Duke tried to stammer an explanation, but Matthews

wasn't in a listening mood. "You heard me! Get out! If you can't hustle, we don't want you!"

Duke tried hard to fight back the hot, angry tears. He hadn't come three thousand miles to exercise! He turned on his heels and walked quickly away from the enraged coach.

Storming into the barracks, he dragged his suitcase out from under the cot and began stuffing it with his clothes. Then, he stopped, sat down and just stared hard at the floor.

How could he go back home now? What would he tell his mother—and Beverly?

As the minutes passed, his anger turned inward. Finally, he knew what he had to do. He left the building, walked to the office of Branch Rickey, Jr., and knocked.

"Come in."

Duke opened the door and crossed to Rickey's desk. "I'm Duke Snider," he began contritely.

Rickey nodded. "Matthews was just in here. I heard all about you."

"I'd like another chance, Mr. Rickey."

"We can't use a man who doesn't hustle all the time."

"Just let me play ball. Let me show you what I can do."

"We know what you can do." Rickey had Snider's folder on the desk before him. Tom Downey had given the boy an unconditional recommendation, one of the most enthusiastic received at Dodger headquarters. Downey claimed the seventeen-year-old had a perfect swing, legs like steel springs and murderous power at the plate.

[35]

"Has great strength of arm and speed on the bases. Uncanny knack at rushing in gracefully on sinking line drives and clutching them just off the grass."

Rickey looked up from the folder. "According to Downey you're too good to let go. So, let's say we've decided to start over again."

Duke let out a sigh of relief. "Gee, thanks Mr. Rickey. You'll see . . ."

"Show us what you can do next week in the game against West Point."

On a bright spring day in March of 1944, Duke Snider was given his first big chance with the Dodgers. It came in a game against the U. S. Military Academy at West Point on the historic bluffs that overlook the Hudson River.

Duke felt a moment of trepidation when Durocher gave him the nod to start at center field. He knew both Durocher and Rickey would be watching every move, looking for any mistake.

Duke's first play in the outfield came in the second inning. Neither side had scored, but the Cadets now threatened. With two out they had the bases loaded and their clean-up man at the plate.

Alert and ready, Duke waited in the outfield as the batter took a ball, then watched two strikes go by. Duke stood with knees bent, his body weight distributed evenly on the balls of his feet. His hands rested on his knees while his eyes stayed riveted on the batter. It was the stance Coach Matthews called "perfect to get a quick start on a ball."

On the next pitch, the Cadet batter swung and lofted a towering fly ball into the sun.

At the crack of the bat, Duke tapped the peak of his cap and dropped his sunglasses down over his eyes. He was wearing the type used by most major leaguers, a pair of glasses on a band which fits around the head.

Duke's instincts told him this one would go deep. He raced back to the edge of the field, then turned to search the brilliant sky for the tiny sphere. For an instant he saw it and ran swiftly to the right as he shouted, "I've got it!" Then he lost the ball in the sun.

Duke strained to locate it again in the bright sky, then suddenly it popped into view, just above the spot where he had camped. As the ball settled comfortably into his glove, he grabbed it and with a single, smooth motion whirled and fired to the plate.

The Cadet on third had tagged up and was jogging easily down the third base line. Too late he realized his mistake. He sped to the plate only to find Duke's throw ready and waiting in the mitt of Dodger catcher Mickey Owen.

It was a spectacular toss to retire the side. His teammates were full of compliments as Duke hurried in from the outfield toward the bench.

As he dropped down beside outfielder Dixie Walker, Duke glanced over to Durocher. The manager nodded. "Nice play," he called. Duke felt good. Durocher had seen and approved.

[37]

At bat for the first time that inning, Duke drew a walk, but was out on a double play as he slid into second. In the sixth, he came up with a man on first. It was still a scoreless tie.

Duke let the first pitch go by. It cut the corner for a strike. The right-hander pumped and threw a fast one down the middle. Savagely Duke slammed into it. It felt good; this one would go. The tremendous drive sailed over 400 feet, clearing the tennis courts in deep right field. The Dodger bench was on its feet, shouting approval. Duke glowed with confidence as his teammates gave him the customary home-run handshakes and pats on the back.

Duke's powerful blow turned out to be the measure of victory on that memorable day as the Dodgers went on to hold the Cadets to a 2–0 shutout.

That night Duke slept better than he had in a week. At last he had been given an opportunity to prove himself to the Dodger high command. Now, he was confident he would be assigned to an important team in the International League.

But Duke had not reckoned with the vagaries of baseball. Two weeks later, he was shipped to Montreal as a utility outfielder. He came to bat twice as a pinch hitter, failed to get a hit either time, and found himself on a train traveling South. He was being sent to Newport News, Virginia, a Dodger Class B farm team in the Piedmont League.

Jake Pitler, a rough, tough, gray-haired character with a lined, sunburned face, was manager at Newport News.

[38]

Putting Branch Rickey's beardless wonders through their paces was a chore not particularly suited to a man with his quick temper and explosive temperament.

The reporters enjoyed getting under Jake's skin and making him howl. When one of them dubbed the team a "day nursery" it drove Pitler's blood pressure up a couple of points and made life unbearable for the new recruits.

Pitler actually considered himself little more than a glorified baby sitter. He and one of his pitchers were the only men on the club old enough to shave. To keep his players amused during the few idle moments he allowed them, Pitler had one solution: "We carried every comic book ever printed."

Jake's roster actually included two fifteen-year-olds. As it turned out, neither of them ever did make the grade. But among the others in the group were Bobby Morgan, Buddy Hicks, Clem Labine and Steve Lembo, all seventeen; Tommy Brown and Preston Ward, sixteen. All reached the major leagues—an amazing tribute to Branch Rickey's farm system and Jake Pitler's training.

Typical of the problems Jake had been facing was a recent hassle at a Dodger staff meeting. The staff insisted that one of Pitler's pitchers be released. The boy was completely worthless, but Jake refused to let him go.

"Be reasonable," Branch Rickey pleaded. "You're only allowed sixteen men. He can't do you any good. Why keep this one?"

"Because," Jake shouted angrily, "he's the only one old enough to drive the bus!"

And so, to Jake Pitler's "nursery" came another hopeful—Edwin Donald Snider. Jake had little patience with any of his juvenile brood, least of all a new center fielder who resented being sent to Newport in the first place.

Duke resented the small amount of money he was getting—$150 per month—as well as the time wasted in Class B ball. Pitler was not the man to offer much sympathy, and the inevitable explosion between player and manager finally came.

At bat one day with the count three-and-one, Duke caught Pitler's signal to take the next pitch. Duke was furious. He wanted to cut at a good one if it came along, but now he was stymied by Pitler's order. Sure enough, he had to watch a perfect pitch go by, a waist-high fast ball that split the strike zone. With the count now three-and-two, Duke swung at the next pitch, and struck out.

In a rage, he kicked the dirt and angrily tossed his bat into the air. Pitler's strategy had forced him to look at a good pitch and swing at a bad one. As Duke saw it, he had been cruelly victimized and wanted his manager to share the blame. Deep down, he was as angry with himself as he was with Pitler. He had been striking out too many times, particularly against left-handers. As he stormed into the dugout, he kicked over the water bucket.

"That'll cost you ten bucks!" Pitler announced.

In the verbal battle that ensued, tempers rose; angry retort followed angry retort. By the time it was over, and Duke was finally silenced, the little temper tantrum had cost him fifty dollars, a third of his month's salary.

From that day, until the end of the season, Duke contented himself with taking out his aggression on opposing pitchers. Though Newport finished the 1944 season in last place, Duke's .294 average was fifth highest in the league among those playing 100 or more games. He led the league with 34 doubles and 9 home runs. All in all, it was a highly respectable performance for a seventeen-year-old on his first time around in the pro leagues.

But it became painfully clear to Duke that he had to overcome his one big problem: left-handed pitching. He had struck out 96 times!

This gave him something real to worry about, and as he was inclined to do at such times, he sank into a morass of self-doubt. Was he *really* pro material? Would he make the majors? Duke thought of his father, off in the South Pacific, and wished he were near at hand to lend support. They had always talked things over, and it had made Duke more sure of himself. That night, he received a letter from his mother informing him that a childhood friend had been killed in action. Now more than ever, Duke wanted to be with his father. The next day, without consulting the Dodger brass, he enlisted in the Navy.

4

●●●●●●●●●●●●●●●●●●●●●●●●●●●●●●●●●●●●●

For Duke Snider, the war was, strangely, a welcome relief—the pressure was off. The Navy had removed him from the fiercely competitive arena of professional baseball, and placed him in a routine, well-regulated existence. He found he could behave like other ordinary eighteen-year-olds. Nobody worried about his batting average, how fast he could run sixty yards or whether he could tell the difference between a ball and a strike. All he was expected to do was be a good sailor—no more, no less.

After spending Christmas of 1944 in boot camp on the West Coast, Duke shipped out aboard the U.S.S. *Sperry,* a submarine tender, for seven months' duty at Pearl Harbor. He followed that with eleven months of shipping in and out of Guam.

[42]

It was dull, often dirty duty, but Duke never complained. He made fireman second class, grew a few inches taller and filled out across the shoulders. To pass the lonely weeks and months, he kept up a steady stream of correspondence with Beverly Null. Though there wasn't much to report from letter to letter, he could always find something to share with his girl.

They planned the celebration they would have together when he was discharged, right down to the restaurant and the last item on the menu; Duke wrote about his preference for living in California, and his desire one day to own some land. As for Beverly, she indicated her preference for large families and children with blue eyes.

Baseball was rarely mentioned. With a woman's wisdom, Beverly kept Duke's attention directed elsewhere. She knew he wasn't sure where he stood with the Dodgers, or whether they had any plans for him at all.

In May of 1946, after eighteen months of service, Edwin Donald Snider received his honorable discharge from the United States Navy.

Duke returned to California, had his celebration with his mother and Beverly, then waited for the Dodgers to call him. While he waited, he put on his semipro uniform and began to work out with his old Montebello team. One day, he became aware that he was being watched. The man doing the watching had been at the ball park all week. Finally, he came over and introduced himself as a scout for the Pittsburgh Pirates. If Duke was a free agent, the Pirates were prepared to pay him $15,000 to sign a contract!

[43]

Duke asked the man to repeat the amount, although he had heard him the first time. But he was still the legal property of the Dodgers and not free to accept any offers.

Then, when he was beginning to feel frustrated and caged, the phone call came from Brooklyn, and Duke went into Los Angeles for a meeting with Branch Rickey, Jr.

"How have you been, Duke?"

"Good," Duke said as he pumped Rickey's hand. He remembered their meeting two years ago at Bear Mountain. He had been a green kid, and Rickey had given him "another chance." Since then, he had come to feel the Dodgers never would have thrown him out of camp. It had all been a trick to get a young rookie into line. He smiled to himself. You live and learn. It was a part of growing up.

"Ready to climb back into uniform?" Rickey asked.

"That's why I'm here." Duke grinned.

"Good," Rickey said, and began to shuffle through a stack of papers. "You're probably a little rusty. Guess it'd be best to bring you up slow."

There it was—the old squeeze play. Rickey had something up his sleeve. Duke parried, "Been playing with the old team in Montebello. Got most of the kinks out."

"Still," Rickey argued, "it's more than eighteen months since you've had on a baseball uniform."

"The Pirates offered me fifteen thousand to sign a contract." Duke paused as Rickey's eyebrows went up. "Too bad I'm not a free agent."

The Dodger executive got the point and began to re-shuffle the papers on his desk. Clearly, Rickey didn't relish telling Duke what was on his mind. "We've been over your case at length. The consensus is another year at Newport News."

Duke kept both his voice and temper under control as he said quietly, but firmly, "I want Class A ball *this* year—or I don't play."

Though the Dodger executive could have threatened to bar him from organized baseball if he didn't obey orders, Rickey was smart enough to know the time had come to offer a compromise.

"Just had an idea," he said.

Duke smiled.

"Ray Hayworth down at Fort Worth might be able to use you in utility. It's the only spot open in Class A."

"I'll be on the next train!"

In Fort Worth, Duke found still-another disappointment. The only spot Hayworth had for him was on the bench; the line-up had already been set.

In short order, the enthusiasm with which he had left Los Angeles evaporated. He became bitter and morose. Called upon only to pinch-hit, his average stayed under .200.

Hayworth had resented having to take the rookie in the first place. Now he had seen quite enough to convince him that Snider didn't belong in Class A ball. He called Duke over one day.

"Snider," the manager said, shaking his head, "I'm sending you back to Newport News."

"You haven't given me a chance to prove myself," Duke complained.

"What're you going to prove?"

Duke looked Hayworth squarely in the eye. "That I'm good enough to stay."

"You'd better prove it by the end of the week." And with that Hayworth turned and walked away.

Duke proved it that very night when he hit two home runs.

After the game, Coach Hayworth spoke the sweetest words Duke had heard in a long time.

"I'm moving you into the starting line-up tomorrow. Keep it up and the spot's yours for good."

With a chance to play the outfield and come to bat in regular rotation, Duke's spirits soared, as did his batting average. By the season's end, he had driven his average up more than sixty points, and led Fort Worth into the championship playoffs against Dallas for the Texas League crown.

In the stands sat Dodger coach Clyde Sukeforth, a man who could change Duke's life. He had been asked to send back a report on the California rookie.

Sukeforth watched with interest that turned to delight as young Snider belted four home runs in six games, to give Fort Worth the title and Duke the batting honors. One of his homers had zoomed out and up with a jet take-off, clearing the clock above the right-center-field fence with plenty to spare. The clock stood 430 feet from home plate!

Sukeforth knew he was watching a picture-book hitter with the kind of home run power that becomes a great gate attraction.

At the next Dodger staff meeting, a highly optimistic Sukeforth reported his findings: "Ted Williams can't even carry his glove."

The Duke was on his way.

It was a jubilant twenty-year-old who left California in the spring of 1947 to join the Dodgers at their training camp in Havana, Cuba. Duke really hustled in an all-out effort to assure himself of an assignment to a Class AAA team.

What Duke couldn't possibly know was that he had already been selected for bigger things. Branch Rickey himself began the publicity build-up at a press conference in the luxurious Hotel Nacional de Cuba.

Recalling Tom Downey's description of the rookie's attributes, the Dodger president announced to an assemblage of sports writers that his new sensation had "a perfect swing," "legs made of steel springs," and was the equal of Stan Musial, the National League's current batting champion. Musial had closed out the 1946 season with a sizzling .365 average.

The reporters filled their columns with Rickey's high praise, and fed it back to the Brooklyn fans, who ate it up. As for Duke, the "star billing" went to his head.

He was coming through the hotel lobby one morning

when Harold Parrott, the club's traveling secretary, walked up to him.

"What've you been eating in the dining room?" Parrott wanted to know. "Pheasant under glass?"

Duke looked puzzled and Parrott produced the food bill—$150 for one week!

"Ever hear of Shanty Hogan?" Parrott asked.

Duke shook his head.

"Hogan could eat a six-pound roast and drink ten bottles of beer in one sitting. Keep on like this and you're going to make baseball forget Hogan."

Parrott stormed out of the hotel, and Duke decided to stop believing the things he read about himself in the papers and curb his recently acquired taste for filet mignon.

As Duke walked toward the players' entrance to Ebbets Field, he tried to appear casual but excitement surged inside him. This clear, crisp April day would be his first in the majors. Proudly, he walked through the gate and headed for the Dodger clubhouse.

He found John Griffin, the team's equipment manager, waiting. The kindly old man who had been with the Dodgers since 1917 had set aside a uniform with the number four on it.

"You got any superstitions against that number?" he asked.

"Nope. Good as any other I guess."

Griffin looked thoughtfully at the number and shook

his head. "You're wrong. It's better than most. Belonged to Dolph Camilli. Remember him?"

"Sure! He's from California, too. Used to play first base."

"Hit thirty-four home runs for us in forty-one," Griffin recalled. "Think you can do as good?"

"Try my best," Duke said as he ran his fingers across the soft flannel.

"I've been saving that number for a long-ball hitter like Dolph. I hear you might be him."

"I hope so," Duke said as he hurried toward the locker room.

He changed quickly, tucked his glove in his back pocket and started out for the playing field.

On this great day Duke would be joining a team that many considered tops in the National League. The infield included Pee Wee Reese at short, Eddie Stanky at second, with Johnny Jorgensen and Cookie Lavagetto sharing third base honors. Bruce Edwards behind the plate caught such big guns as Ralph Branca, Vic Lombardi, Rex Barney and Joe Hatten, with Hugh Casey in the bullpen. In the outfield the competition was fierce. Dixie Walker, Pete Reiser and Gene Hermanski were already rotating with Carl Furillo. Duke tried not to think about that too much, for he knew it left him on the outside looking in. And to make matters worse, Durocher, who had seen Duke in action and liked what he saw, wouldn't be at the Brooklyn helm for the '47 season.

A week earlier Leo Durocher had been suspended

from baseball for a full year, the climax to a feud with baseball commissioner Happy Chandler. The loss of the colorful, quick-tempered Durocher could be a serious blow to the Dodgers' pennant hopes. To Duke it meant the loss of a "friend in court." Who would the new manager be? So far Branch Rickey was keeping fans and reporters guessing. He had more immediate problems on this opening day of 1947.

Ebbets Field, jammed to the rafters, was now the tense and anxious setting for a historic event in the annals of baseball. Rickey had the first Negro in the major leagues playing for the Dodgers: Jackie Robinson at first base.

Duke took his place on the bench, as the Braves and Dodgers hurried onto the field. With the rest of the fans, he focused his attention on Robinson. He knew of Jackie's exploits at U.C.L.A. and up at Montreal, but playing at Ebbets Field was something else again.

Would Jackie prove equal to the task of major league competition? Duke knew that that was what the fans were there to see.

In the course of the game, Jackie grounded to third, flied out, hit into a double play, was safe on an error and was finally yanked in the ninth for defensive purposes.

As for Duke, he wasn't even called on to hit in what turned out to be a 5–3 victory over the Braves.

Next day, with Si Johnson on the mound for Boston, Robinson got his first hit, a bunt single. Duke felt better. Now he had only himself to worry about. As the innings slipped by, he kept telling himself he would get his chance. It came late in the game with the Dodgers well out in front.

The sound of his name announced over the loud-speaker for the first time in Ebbets Field was a thrill for Duke. He set himself at the plate to wait for Johnson's first pitch. Knee-high, it snapped in for a strike. Duke stepped back, tapped the dirt from his spikes and straightened his cap. Johnson pumped and sent a breaking curve toward the plate. Duke met it squarely and drove the ball into the outfield for his first major-league hit, a line-drive single.

The following day the Dodgers moved over to the Polo Grounds for a series with the Giants. Rickey used the occasion to bring in his new manager, sixty-three-year-old, white-haired Burt Shotton. A veteran Dodger scout, Shotton had been coaxed out of semiretirement in Florida. And, as Duke had feared, he would now be managed by a man who had never seen him in action.

Brooklyn gave their new skipper a rousing 10–4 victory over the Giants, but Duke was still on the bench. That day he didn't even get up to pinch-hit.

The Dodgers were off to a flying start, and the quiet Shotton, in sharp contrast to the bombastic Durocher, proved to be an excellent field general. But Duke went practically unnoticed, the victim of an overstaffed outfield.

Each passing day heightened his frustrations. If he wasn't going to be given a chance why had they called him up in the first place? After three weeks of warming the bench, Duke went in to see the general manager.

"Mr. Rickey," he announced, "I'd like to be farmed out."

"What's the problem?"

"I want to play ball—not sit on the bench waiting to pinch-hit."

Rickey nodded. He was fully aware of the problem. On a weaker team, Snider would be playing regularly. "We're overstocked," he admitted.

"After all the stuff you said in the papers, I expected to be playing every day."

"You will. Don't worry. And, Duke . . ." Rickey paused to let his words sink in, "I believe the things I said."

"I wish you hadn't started comparing me to Musial."

"The reporters on your back?"

Duke nodded. "If I'm so good, they want to know why I'm not in there regularly."

"Well, don't let it get you. I didn't say you'd beat Musial out this season, did I? Have a little faith, Duke. I've got a pretty good crystal ball. Look at Robinson. My instincts were right about him. Unless I miss my guess, he'll lead us to a pennant and turn out to be Rookie of the Year."

"Sure looks like it, Mr. Rickey."

"Then don't argue with me about how good I think you are!" Duke smiled and the Old Man continued. "I'm pleased you want to be farmed out. Under the circumstances, it shows a mature, intelligent attitude."

Rickey came out from behind his desk and placed an arm around Duke's shoulder. "You're growing up. It's what I like to see."

Duke hadn't been spoken to with such kindness in years. He mumbled simply, "Thank you, Mr. Rickey."

Rickey explained that in leaving Brooklyn, Duke would be losing his right to any World Series money—if the Dodgers went on to take the pennant, as now seemed likely.

"I wouldn't be earning my share by sitting on the bench. I never did like charity."

"What about Beverly Null? What's she going to say?"

Duke's eyes widened with amazement. How did the boss know about her?

Rickey smiled. "We keep close watch. Especially on you younger men. You're valuable property. Takes a good woman to protect it. You planning to marry the girl?"

"Just as soon as I can afford it."

"All right, then here's the deal," Rickey declared. "I'll send you to St. Paul. No matter what happens there, don't worry. I'll see that you get a one-quarter share of any Series money."

Duke shook hands, wired his folks and Beverly his new address and took the next train for Minnesota.

With St. Paul of the American Association, Duke had his wish. As the team's regular center fielder, he played every day. He roared through sixty-six games driving in forty-six runs with twenty-two doubles, seven triples and twelve home runs. His batting average was a good .316. He might have won Rookie of the Year of the American Association—which went to Alvin Dark of Milwaukee—but for a summons back to Brooklyn in late season. He was ineligible to play in the World Series, but he could be on hand to watch and cheer.

As Rickey predicted, the Dodgers had swept to the pennant, and Jackie Robinson had been named Rookie of the Year by the St. Louis *Sporting News*, the baseball "Bible." The Old Man seemed to have an uncanny knack for calling the turns, and Duke hoped Rickey's prophecies would be as accurate when it came to him.

In the World Series, it was the highly touted Yankees against the Dodgers. What many thought would be a pushover turned out to be a bitter struggle right down to the seventh and final game before the Yankees edged out Brooklyn and locked up another World Championship

Brooklyn had made a mighty stand, far better than had been anticipated, and Duke headed back for a winter in California proud of his team and confident he would participate in the next Series.

He was equally pleased with Branch Rickey's farewell. The Old Man handed him an envelope. "This is for you and Beverly," he said. "Call her and set the date."

Duke opened the envelope. It contained a one-quarter player's share of the Dodgers' World Series money: $1,020.

"Thanks . . . thanks, Mr. Rickey," Duke stammered.

Rickey grinned. "Get out of here and call your girl!"

Duke did call Beverly. And on October 25, 1947, Duke Snider and Beverly Null became man and wife, and solved the postwar housing shortage by setting up married life in a two-room trailer.

5

Duke arrived at the Dodger's 1948 training camp in the Dominican Republic filled with a winter of wedded bliss and bubbling with springtime enthusiasm. A week later, he was sullenly pacing back and forth in Branch Rickey's office while the white-haired Brooklyn chieftain announced: "Duke, I don't think you can tell the difference between a ball and a strike."

Rickey had watched his twenty-one-year-old hopeful cut at one bad pitch after another. Finally he decided to do something about it. "You're going to Vero Beach for a special course."

"But, Mr. Rickey . . ."

The wise old man shook his head. "No sense arguing. Remember, I said you'd do better than Musial—someday. Now don't make me out to be a liar. Get on the next plane. George Sisler will be waiting for you."

Duke started to say something, thought better of it, then turned and walked out. Rickey had pointed up the one real weakness that might prevent his getting a regular outfield berth. Eager to pound every pitch over the right-field fence, Duke had a tendency to swing at them all. He needed to learn to control his swing, especially against a curve ball served up by a left-handed pitcher.

As Duke's plane sped north along the Florida coast, he wondered what George Sisler would say and do.

When it came to listing baseball greats, Sisler had to be counted among them. Now a minor league coach, he had placed his name in the players' record book at the end of the 1922 season. His average that year was a fantastic .420, equaling the modern record set by the immortal Ty Cobb in 1911. (Two years later, Rogers Hornsby beat the Cobb-Sisler record with a .424 for the 1924 season, and that record stands to this day.) George Sisler no doubt knew all the batting tricks, Duke had to admit, but that didn't make him feel any better about being sent to Vero Beach.

Next morning as Duke rode to the ball park with Sisler, the veteran turned the conversation to "the good old days" when he played against Ty Cobb.

"Cobb was the best," Sisler maintained. "In twenty-four years, he set ninety records." The aging Sisler thought a moment with half-closed eyes as he brought back the image of his old friend. "You know, Duke, that man played in 3,033 games and hit 3,052 singles—along with a mess of doubles, triples and home runs. He had a

[57]

lifetime batting average of .368, and it has never been topped."

Duke nodded. He knew Cobb's lifetime average. He even knew Sisler's: .340. What he didn't know was the point George Sisler was trying to make.

"Cobb had one secret," the Brooklyn coach concluded. " 'It's knowing what to hit,' he used to say."

Duke got the point. "I guess that's my problem."

"Admitting it is half the battle. The other half you leave to me."

Twice a day, Duke stood at the plate, hands at his side, while George Sisler watched from behind the batter's cage. On the mound stood an electronic pitching machine that coughed up balls as directed. For the first twenty minutes Duke simply stood and judged each pitch. "Good" or "bad" he would say, with Sisler checking him on the accuracy of each call.

Then Sisler set the machine for the low inside pitch. When thrown as a change-up or low-speed curve, it was invariably a bad ball. During the next twenty minutes Duke swung at the offerings served up by the tireless pitching machine.

The "special course" proved only one thing: Snider had as good an eye as Sisler or anyone else while in training. It didn't prove what he would or would not do under competitive conditions.

One lesson Duke Snider *did* learn at Vero Beach. It came from watching Pete Reiser, the twenty-nine-year-old switch-hitting outfielder who had led the league in 1941 with a .343 average.

Reiser was at Vero taking a course, too. He was trying to learn to play first base. Duke wondered why, and asked George Sisler.

"Pete's run into a lot of fences trying to catch home runs. The battering has about caught up with him."

During an exhibition game at Vero, Reiser stepped up to the plate and walloped the ball for a triple—or what should have been a triple. Halfway between second and third base, he fell down. As Duke watched, he knew that Pete's legs had simply given out under him and that he was seeing an outfielder who was washed up before he was thirty. Duke would never allow himself to forget that sight: Reiser crumpling to the ground because of the battering he had taken against the fences of ball parks around the country. Duke Snider vowed then and there never to allow himself to make the same mistake in the outfield.

The training course had publicized Snider's major batting problem and neither the Brooklyn brain trust nor the sports writers were inclined to forget about it.

Leo Durocher, now rehired by Rickey after his year's suspension, was not a manager to take a batting weakness lightly. Durocher believed in attacking a problem head-on.

Determined to make a comeback, Leo wanted a top team. The previous year, Shotton had won the pennant. Leo had decided to do as well—and that did not include carrying a left-handed batter who could not hit left-handed pitchers, much as he admired Duke's potential at the plate.

As the 1948 season got under way, Durocher threw Snider at every left-handed pitcher in the league. His strategy was simple: "If left-handers give you trouble, keep facing them until you got them beat."

The tormented Snider was given little respite, and Duke, who had so admired Durocher, now began to hate his guts. Durocher seemed to be waiting for another left-hander to appear just so he could throw Duke at him. The constant harping on the same problem kept Duke on edge. Instead of helping, the Durocher technique only hindered and really gave him something to worry about. He developed into a steady strike-out victim. And the more he pressed, the less effective he became. Rarely did Durocher allow him the luxury of blasting the right-handers. That would have offset Duke's bad days against the southpaws, but Leo wasn't about to let him relax.

In Philadelphia, Duke did manage to hit a pair of homers off rookie Curt Simmons, but the veteran left-handers—Pollet and Brecheen of St. Louis, Schmitz of Chicago, Raffensberger of Cincinnati—had his number.

Duke and the Dodgers fumbled along on their second division treadmill, while Manager Durocher grew more fretful and irascible.

Leo's position with the Dodgers was rapidly deteriorating, and to arouse flagging team spirit, he tried a grand-stand play. He put Jackie Robinson on the waiver list. The announcement that the Dodgers would consider trading the highly regarded Robinson was merely a tactic to spur the team into greater action. But no one believed the ruse, and Brooklyn continued to perform badly.

As for Snider, *he* could be sacrificed to show that Leo meant business, and so on May 17, Duke was handed a one-way ticket to Montreal with orders to report to Clay Hopper.

Snider's departure failed to improve conditions for the Dodger manager. Finally, he moved over to manage the New York Giants, and Rickey brought back Burt Shotton to take over the faltering Dodgers for the remainder of the season.

Meanwhile, up in Montreal, Duke turned his hostility and aggression on the entire International League. His unhappy experience with Durocher had left him high-strung and overanxious, and as a result he was trying too hard.

He did everything with intensity as if striking back at Leo, and this need for revenge almost became his undoing. In an attempt to snag a short fly ball, Duke collided with infielder Jimmy Bloodworth and suffered a severe spike wound below the right shin. The bleeding persisted, and Duke was taken to the hospital.

At this point in his life, he could not have been more despondent. His career seemed to have touched rock bottom. A married man with responsibilities, he refused to delude himself about his future prospects. Before Durocher had sent him to Montreal, the reporters had begun calling him "the strike-out kid." And last season Rickey had compared him to Musial! Now, here he was, flat on his back, waiting for the doctor to pronounce sentence.

"You should be as good as new in about three weeks."

"Can't you make it a little sooner?" the impatient Snider pleaded.

The doctor shook his head, gave instructions to the nurse and left Duke to adjust to the antiseptic white-walled hospital room. The only bright note was the doctor's parting remark to the nurse: "Give him anything he wants to eat."

Duke tried to read, managed to write a reassuring letter home to Beverly and his parents, but there were still too many hours to think. His cold-blooded analysis of the situation left him completely dejected. He refused to call it "bad luck" or "fate." He blamed himself. Here he was building a marriage and a future on a career that simply wouldn't get started.

"You look about as low as a hound dog who lost his first possum!"

Duke looked up to find Cliff Dapper, a catcher and fellow Californian, the best friend he had on the Montreal team, standing in the doorway of the hospital room with a box in his hands and a grin on his face.

"Thought this might cheer you up," Dapper said as he set the box down and carefully began to unwrap it.

"What have you got in there?" Duke wanted to know.

"California gold!" Dapper removed the outer wrapper to disclose a small wooden crate. "Since you can eat what you like, I've brought you the fruit of the gods." Prying open the top of the small crate, Dapper pulled aside

some straw stuffing and removed a ripe, beautifully pro-
portioned avocado. "Had it flown in from my ranch in
California!" he announced proudly. Dapper owned two
and a half acres in Whittier.

Duke couldn't help laughing. "You are a fool, Cliff!"

"Made you laugh, didn't I?" Dapper countered.
"That's more than Durocher could do. Proves I'm
smarter." He placed the green fruit in Duke's hand.
"Now you eat some of my homegrown avocado, mixed
with a little garlic, and I guarantee it'll cure what ails
you."

With Cliff to keep him company, Duke forgot about
himself. They talked mostly about Dapper's avocado
"ranch."

"When I'm too old to hit that ball," Cliff said, "and
too tired to chase around those bases, I'll have a place to
go to that's all mine. Nothing makes you feel better than
knowing the earth beneath your feet belongs to you.
Take care of it, and it pays you back with something
good to eat. Can't ask for much more."

As Duke listened to his friend, a new image began to
evolve. It was a dream built upon adult awareness and
adult needs. As a youngster, he had wanted to become
a big league star and play in a World Series. But now, as
a man, his dream was for something substantial, something he could call his own—land.

Whenever Cliff came to visit Duke, they spent the
time talking about the price of avocados and the relative
merits of various fertilizers. In three weeks, Duke knew
everything Dapper did about avocado farming—and so

did Beverly. He reported the day's avocado seminar in long letters each night.

Gradually, the bitterness and the frustration of confinement disappeared. A vitality and anticipation took its place. Duke could scarcely wait to climb back into uniform. Now he wanted success, not for itself, but for the things it could bring, the things he and Cliff Dapper had been talking about.

On the night before he was discharged from the hospital, Duke said, "Cliff, have you ever thought about a partnership?"

"Who'd you have in mind?" Dapper asked.

"You and me," Duke replied.

Dapper grinned. "Why do you think I've been talking my fool head off?"

The two men shook hands and promised that one day, together, they would plant and then harvest the biggest crop of avocados ever.

With a vengeance Duke returned to battle under the Montreal banner, tearing apart International League pitching at a .327 clip. Though he was averaging two bases on each hit, Manager Clay Hopper refused to believe his eyes. One day, with two men on base, none out and the score tied, Hopper flashed Duke the bunt signal.

Duke's leg was still sore from the inflammation, and dropping a bunt meant he would have to race down the line. A long hit would give him more running time, and he had been walloping the ball in all directions.

Hopper flashed the bunt signal again. Duke turned

away, set his feet firmly at the plate and hit the next pitch for a home run. As the ball cleared the right-field fence, Duke trotted leisurely around the bases.

As he rounded third, the irate Hopper gave his star the usual congratulatory handshake. What the shouting fans didn't hear was Hopper's remark. "That does it! Pay the office fifty!"

When one of the reporters questioned Hopper after the game, the Montreal manager declared: "I'd like to shoot him for disobeying a sign, but I have no other power hitter."

Duke wasn't around to explain how much the injured leg still pained him, and Hopper's statement grabbed the headlines.

In New York, the story brought a smile to Branch Rickey's face. Snider's audacity gave him one of the few bright moments he had during the dismal 1948 season. Brooklyn was floundering; Montreal, with Snider in the attack, was on top.

The Dodger president called in his son. "Get up to Montreal. Find out how angry the fans would be if we took Duke Snider away."

6

●●●●●●●●●●●●●●●●●●●●●●●●●●●●●●●●●●●

No sooner had Branch Rickey sent his son off to Montreal than he set the second part of his plan into motion. At a cost of $5,000, he arranged for Sam Jethroe, a star of the Negro American League, to step into Duke's place in Montreal.

Rickey desperately needed Snider's power at the plate. Under Shotton's skillful guidance, the Dodgers had inched forward, battling out of the second division into a challenging position for the pennant. Now, in August, Brooklyn held a tenuous grip on first place. Duke might just make the difference as the Dodgers surged down the home stretch.

From Montreal, Rickey Junior reported that Montreal, in contention for the International League flag, also needed Snider. "He poled one out of the park today, the longest homer in twenty years up here. That makes forty-four runs he's driven in in seventy-seven games."

With a broad grin, Rickey turned to Burt Shotton who was seated opposite him. "He hit another one today. If we pull him out, they're liable to burn down the stadium."

"If you don't, we're liable to lose a pennant."

Rickey turned back to his phone. "No announcements. No press conferences. Nothing," he advised his son. "**Get Snider out tonight and bring him home!**"

Duke finished buttoning his shirt with the big number four on it, set his cap on his head and shut the locker door.

"This is it!" he told himself. "This time it's for keeps. My second try at Ebbets Field. Three and you're out. Well, he would make it in two."

"Good luck, Duke!" called Pee Wee Reese, the Kentucky farmboy who had developed into the game's greatest shortstop.

"Good to be back!" Duke said and meant it.

Then up came Roy Campanella to say hello. Campanella had been brought up earlier in the season from St. Paul to fill the team's catching needs.

"Campy helped boost us out of the cellar," Reese said. "Maybe you can keep us up on top."

The Dodgers had been in last place when Campanella joined the team. Now they were in first.

"Let's go after that World Series money!" Campy said

to Snider with a slap on the back. "I got four kids to support!"

"Let's move!" Reese called to the players around him, and the Dodgers started noisily from the clubhouse.

As Duke stepped into the sunlight, he sensed a tenseness in the air. Somehow, Brooklyn was always different —especially on a day the Dodgers played the Giants. There was more vitality. More electricity. With Durocher now managing the Giants, after spending the first part of the season with the Dodgers, every Dodger-Giant encounter took on added spice.

Each team had its turn at batting practice, then the fans set up a rhythmic pattern of clapping and stamping, demanding impatiently that the game get under way.

The groundskeepers finished smoothing out the infield dirt and marking the foul lines. Finally the Dodgers tumbled from the dugout and applause crackled across Ebbets Field. Over the public address system came the time-honored announcement:

"Ladies and gentlemen, our organist Miss Gladys Gooding will now sing the national anthem."

It *was* different in Brooklyn. And, win or lose, it *was* good to be back.

Unfortunately, the Dodgers dropped three in a row to Durocher's men and never recovered from the triple defeat. The battle between Durocher and Rickey, a weak pitching staff and the constant shifting of line-ups all played their part in the downfall of the 1948 Dodgers.

Though Shotton had maneuvered Brooklyn to a pennant in '47, he replaced Durocher too late in the season to salvage the '48 campaign. The quiet, white-haired Shotton had to settle for a third-place niche at season's end, behind the pennant-winning Braves and the St. Louis Cardinals. At least the Dodgers had outplayed Durocher's Giants—and to Duke that was almost as good as taking the flag.

One day, early the following spring, the Dodger hierarchy set the season's master strategy for what they hoped would be a Brooklyn pennant in '49.

Seated about Rickey were Dodger coaches and scouts George Sisler, Clyde Sukeforth, John Carey and Jake Pitler. Rickey glanced down at some penciled notes, removed the ever-present cigar from his mouth and announced the first item on the agenda: "Team captain."

Rickey declared that Pee Wee Reese was the logical choice, the oldest player in point of service and therefore entitled to the extra $500 a player received for serving as team captain. There was no argument, and that point was quickly settled.

Next came a discussion of Gil Hodges fate at first base. His hitting was spotty. They talked about a rookie kid named Chuck Connors as a possible alternative, and about trying to buy aging Johnny Mize from the New York Giants. In the end, Rickey decided to stick with Hodges at first.

When the talk got around to Snider, Sukeforth, who invariably waxed eloquent whenever Duke's name was mentioned, suggested that their prize center fielder be kept away from left-handed pitching.

"Just because you once said he was better than Ted Williams," Burt Shotton declared, "is no reason I have to start coddling him to prove you're right."

The others in the room laughed. But Sukeforth warned: "Just don't pull another Durocher."

During spring training nothing was said to Duke about his perennial batting weakness. The deliberate omission brought it back to Duke's attention. When he mentioned his anxieties to Sukeforth, the Dodger coach said, "Duke, you're wearing Dolph Camilli's number and that ought to mean something to you. In forty-one he set the club's all-time strike-out record, a hundred and fifteen, but that was the year he won the Most Valuable Player Award."

Duke walked away smiling. And it was with a sense of well-being that he approached the new season.

A record crowd of 34,530 jammed Ebbets Field to witness the opening-day battle of 1949 between the Dodgers and the Giants. In a real rout, the Dodgers took it 10–3 and were off to a flying start.

With Shotton in charge from the beginning, plus enough strength in depth to allow players to stay put in one position, the Dodgers surged forward with pennant aspirations. For insurance, Brooklyn had an ace in the hole: a strong rookie hurler named Don Newcombe.

It looked good. This might be the season he actually played in a World Series, Duke thought—the boyhood dream come true. As kid stuff it sounded corny, but now it stood within the realm of possibility. As the dream came closer to reality, Duke began to press, and by mid-summer he was in a full-fledged hitting slump. The Dodgers were stumbling in the pennant race, and mild-mannered Shotton began to lose his temper.

The left-handed curve, the demon that had caused Duke more than one sleepless night, returned to haunt him. In desperation, he finally asked Shotton to let him sit out a game when a left-handed pitcher was on the mound. In Chicago, an angry Burt Shotton sounded off to the press.

"Only two of my outfielders, Snider and Furillo, are worth anything. The rest are a bunch of semipros, but at least they try. Snider doesn't want to hit against left-handers, and Furillo doesn't want to hit against right-handers. How can we win a pennant with that type of playing?"

Shotton's blast received widespread press coverage, and drove Snider into a funk. His back against the wall, Duke turned to a man with a sharp eye and a nimble mind, a man he could call a friend, pitcher Carl Erskine.

"Carl, watch me when I'm hitting good and see how I do it. When I'm hitting bad, tell me what I'm not doing —and what I'm doing that I didn't do before," he begged.

It sounded complicated, but Erskine understood. He knew that the best medicine for Duke was simply having someone sympathetic to talk to.

"I worry too much," the harried Snider admitted. "I keep telling myself everything is going to be all right.

But when you don't feel right, you never get your share of hits."

Erskine nodded. He knew how it was. A pitcher has his bad days, too. Then, all of a sudden, one day you're comfortable and you can't do anything wrong.

Erskine gave Duke a friendly pat on the back. "You forget about the way you hit. For the next few days, leave it to me. I'll keep watch."

At the end of the week, Erskine made his report. "You seem to be taking your eye off the ball," he told Snider. To make the point clear, Erskine showed Duke several photographs he had clipped from a magazine. One showed Duke at his best, the others at his worst.

Pointing to the first photo, Erskine observed: "Here you are hitting a home run. Your left shoulder is up. The bat is straight out in front, and you're looking in a straight line with your shoulder and bat."

Duke stared at the photograph of himself and agreed. The other pictures, taken as he struck out, told a completely different story. Duke could see that his stance was entirely wrong. His left shoulder was down. The bat was off to one side, and he was looking up at the sky.

"I can see the differences," he said to Erskine. "I never noticed it before. Thanks."

"All I can do is point it out. The rest is up to you."

The next day, Duke belted one over the fence, and the slump was over. Whether it was the photographs or just talking to Erskine and finding a sympathetic ear, he never really knew. He began hitting at a furious .400

pace during September, and brought his home run total for the year up to twenty-three.

With a little over a week remaining to the season, and the Dodgers one and a half games out of first place, the league-leading Cardinals began printing their World Series tickets.

Then, the Cardinals dropped four in a row. Suddenly, the Dodgers were on top, leading the league by a full game on the last day of the season.

On the final day, the Dodgers battled the Phillies. If they lost and the Cardinals won, the two teams would wind up in a dead heat and force a playoff—exactly as had occurred back in 1946. And that time, the Dodgers had lost to the Cardinals in the playoffs. The specter of a repeat performance haunted every member of the team.

As the Dodger bout got under way in Philadelphia, Duke and his teammates kept an anxious eye on the scoreboard for results of the Cardinals' closing game.

Through seven innings the Dodgers fought to capture the lead and failed. As they came to bat in the bottom of the eighth, they were trailing 6–4. Then, the scoreboard flashed and the crowd roared. The Cardinals had won their game. Now the Dodgers *had* to win to avoid a play-off for the 1949 pennant.

With Curt Simmons on the mound for Philadelphia, Hodges singled to lead off the Dodger eighth, then Campanella doubled, and pinch-hitter Luis Olmo singled to drive in two runs and tie up the game at 6–6, Reese sacrificed Olmo to second and Jorgensen popped up.

Duke moved to the plate, straightened his cap and told

[73]

himself, "This is it," as Simmons caught the signal from Andy Seminick. Simmons fired and Duke swung. The crack of the bat against the ball brought every fan in the ball park to his feet screaming. Duke raced around first and went into second standing up as Olmo crossed the plate with the tie-breaking run.

Jim Konstanty came in for Philadelphia to put out the fire, and closed the inning by forcing Robinson to pop up. In the top of the ninth, the Phillies pushed in a run to tie it at 7–7. Again, the shadow of a playoff cast its darkened image over the Dodgers as the game moved into extra innings.

The Phillies failed to add any runs in the top of the tenth, and once again it was the Dodgers' turn.

Now Duke noticed with a pang of anxiety that a left-hander, Ken Heintzelman, had taken the mound for Philadelphia. With two out and two on, it was his turn to bat. The fans were clapping for a hit, and the rhythmic sounds seemed to be saying, "a left-hander, a left-hander." Duke felt that everyone in the stadium knew what he was thinking, what he feared and hoped wouldn't happen. If he allowed Heintzelman to strike him out he would never forgive himself. All he needed was a hit. Just long enough to score Reese from second.

Duke glanced toward the on-deck circle where Robinson was kneeling. Jackie smiled and nodded as if to say, "Get rid of the doubt. Don't let the fear plague you. Tell yourself you can do it."

Heintzelman pumped, pitched and Duke let it go by for a ball.

"Wait for a good one!" Robinson called.

Heintzelman shook off a sign from Seminick, then went into his windup and sent the ball twisting toward the plate. A curve from a left-hander. Duke knew it would be coming and was ready. He leveled on the ball and slashed it deep into right field for a hit. Two runs crossed the plate. With a 9–7 win, the Dodgers took another pennant.

Duke Snider was the proudest man in Brooklyn! The crazy kid's dream had come true. Edwin Donald Snider would actually play in his first World Series: the Dodgers versus the Yankees.

Duke wired Beverly to bring his folks to New York for opening day. He tried to act his age, but he couldn't curb his excitement. Suddenly he had become the idol of every Brooklyn fan. The faithful followed him everywhere he went.

"You have to believe in fairy tales," he told Beverly, "when a thing like this can happen!"

Beverly and Mrs. Snider thrilled to Duke's success. But the worldly-wise Ward Snider tried to bring his high-flying son down to earth. "Keep both feet on the ground," he advised. "There aren't any fairy godmothers. Take my word for it."

For the third time in ten years, the World Series found the Dodgers pitted against the Bronx Bombers. The Yankees had taken the 1941 and 1947 series, but Duke and his teammates were determined not to permit a repeat performance. This was the year they would dump Casey Stengel's stalwarts from their position of legendary supremacy. Duke never faced a challenge with greater confidence. Even the skills of Allie Reynolds, Vic Raschi, Tommy Byrne and Ed Lopat combined, to say nothing of the Yankee's brilliant bull-pen star Joe Page, didn't phase him. Let the right-handers *and* the left-handers come. He'd blast them out of the box!

Duke couldn't have been prouder, with Beverly and his parents in the stands, as he stepped up to face Allie Reynolds in game number one. He went down swinging, and that day Duke Snider struck out three times in a row!

The Dodgers dropped the opener, 1–0. Don Newcombe fought a superb pitching duel against Reynolds for eight scoreless innings only to have Tommy Henrich pole one into the stands for the Yankees in the bottom of the ninth.

Preacher Roe faced Vic Raschi in the second game. Robinson led off the second inning with a double, moved to third on a long foul by Hermanski, then scored on a single by Hodges. The Dodgers took that one 1–0, but Duke was still striking out.

The Yankee steamroller buried the Dodgers in the next three games, and it was all over. The Yankees were on top again and their chief victim had been Duke Snider. In twenty-one trips to the plate, he had collected only three hits. To make matters even worse, Duke had struck out eight times, tying the all-time strike-out record for a five-game Series!

Duke couldn't pack and get back to California fast enough. He had a bad case of postseason miseries. It didn't do much good to be reminded that the record he had tied belonged to one of the greatest hitters of all time, Rogers Hornsby, or that Ted Williams, Hans Wagner and even Ty Cobb had turned in poor World Series performances.

Duke went home with Beverly and his folks. On the train he told his wife, "I don't want to read about the Series, or think about it, or be around where people are talking about it. I wish I could go someplace where they never heard about baseball."

"Forget it!" his father snapped. "There'll always be a next year."

"But, Pop, I had the big chance and blew it. We lost to the Yankees, four games to one. All close. If I had been hitting, we might have won four instead of them."

Ward Snider took a long hard look at his son. "Now, you quit worrying. You can't change a thing!"

Duke knew his father was right. Sure it hurt, but there was a next year.

"Mr. Snider," Beverly reminded her husband with a smile, "you've got more important things to worry about."

Duke nodded. Beverly was right. On November 4, 1949, their first child, Kevin Snider, was born.

7

●●●●●●●●●●●●●●●●●●●●●●●●●●●●●●

"A pay hike!" Branch Rickey, Jr.'s face turned a heated red which belied the February temperature outside his office.

"I've got a big family now," Duke maintained stoutly.

"That son of yours doesn't cost an extra five thousand dollars a year to feed."

"No he doesn't, Mr. Rickey. But he makes me realize that I need the security."

Rickey sensed the change in Duke. He wasn't the brash kid anymore. "You're asking for a sixty per cent raise on a two ninety average."

"Two ninety two," Duke responded calmly, "with twenty-three home runs."

"That still doesn't call for a raise to fourteen thousand."

"Wait 'til September. I'll break three hundred this year." Duke was never more serious in his life. "I want that kid to remember something better than his old man striking out eight times in a World Series."

Duke's self-confidence pleased Rickey. That was what made great ballplayers. Jackie Robinson had it. So did Hodges and Pee Wee Reese. Rickey gave Duke the salary he asked for. If his instincts were right, the extra money would be well invested. Now was certainly no time to discourage Snider.

Duke signed the contract and felt like a new man. The brooding, the sulking disappeared, buried beneath what had been a winter of discontent. Now, for the sake of Beverly and their son, Kevin, he set out to make his mark.

By Decoration Day of the 1950 season, the Dodgers had inched within half a game of the league-leading Phillies. With a holiday double-header scheduled, the faithful flocked to Ebbets Field. In the opener, the Dodgers beat the Phillies, 7–6, and landed in first place by half a game. The victory had been accomplished without much help from their $14,000-a-year center fielder. Duke had gone hitless in five trips to the plate. Before he had time to tell himself he was in a slump, the second game got under way with Jack Banta on the mound for Brooklyn.

In the first inning, three Phillies came up and, just as promptly, three Phillies went down. For the Dodgers, neither Billy Cox nor Gene Hermanski could get the wood on Russ Meyer's sharp deliveries, and that brought up the hapless Duke Snider.

The fans were beginning to ride him. His five hitless trips to the plate in the first game had got them on his back. They wanted action all the time, and they let a ballplayer know it.

"Come on, Duke," he could hear some fan shout, "show 'em you ain't forgotten how to hit!"

"Hey, Snider," another one called, "you want another raise?"

Duke tried to shut out the voices. Sometimes he hated them all. He had promised Rickey he would break .300 and here he was, at the end of May, on the brink of a major slump. He could feel his stomach muscles tighten. And that made him think of his father. "When the tension gets too tight," he could hear him say, "take two deep breaths and let the air out slow."

It used to work for him as a kid. Duke took two deep breaths and exhaled slowly as Russ Meyer began his delivery.

The ball came spinning toward the plate. Duke swung and felt the solid impact as the bat met the ball. The crowd roared their approval as they saw the ball sail over the fence and out into Bedford Avenue.

Light and easy, Duke rounded third and headed home to score the first run of the game. The fans continued their raucous applause until he ducked into the dugout to join his beaming teammates.

Burt Shotton patted him on the back as he went by.

"Give us some more of that," the Dodger manager said, "and you'll be batting in third place for keeps."

Duke had been shifted back and forth in the line-up depending upon who was pitching and how much confidence Shotton had in him on any one day. A permanent slot would mean full approval and acceptance.

Duke's next turn at bat came in the bottom of the third. The Dodgers were now leading, 2–1. As he faced Meyer for the second time, Duke stood loose and easy. The slump was gone. It was a thing you felt and knew.

Meyer snapped in a low inside pitch, then tried for the strike zone with a fast ball. Duke was ready. He met the ball squarely and sent it spinning right where the first one had landed, out into Bedford Avenue.

The delirious fans were shouting themselves hoarse. As Duke touched home plate, half the team was there to meet him.

"Beautiful!" Pee Wee called.

Robinson followed a pat on the seat of the pants with, "You never looked better!"

Duke slipped into the dugout, the wild applause still ringing in his ears.

In the fifth inning, Duke came to bat again. Meyer had been replaced on the mound for the Phillies by Blix Donnelly. As he stood waiting, Duke could hear the fans demanding still another home run.

"Strike one!" Umpire Al Barlick called as the first pitch zipped down the middle with Duke merely watching.

Donnelly threw the next one wide for a ball, but cut the corner with the third pitch for a second strike.

"Blast it over the fence!" the fans screamed. Thirty thousand hysterical voices seemed to be shouting at him to do something. Duke swung on Donnelly's next pitch. The crack of the bat told everyone in Ebbets Field that it was a clean hit. The stadium echoed with the thunderous roar of the delirious crowd as the ball traveled deep to left center, hit a railing in the stands and bounced back onto the playing field.

Duke wasn't sure what had happened. Ashburn had the ball in the outfield, hesitated, then threw toward the plate as Duke raced around third.

Umpire Barlick signaled the hit a homer, but Duke wasn't talking any chances. He slid into home to beat the relay and make sure.

Pandemonium became the order of the day! Three straight homers! The fans pounded, shouted and literally screamed themselves hoarse. Only two other Dodgers had ever hit three home runs in one game: Jack Fournier in 1926 and Gene Hermanski in 1948.

With the adulation of the fans ringing in his ears, Duke picked himself up out of the dust at home plate and grinned sheepishly at umpire Barlick. "I just wanted to make sure," he said by way of explanation.

"I would, too," Barlick replied. As Duke headed toward the dugout, the fans pounded their hands, the benches, each other, and everything else in sight. Each member of the Dodger team came over to shake Duke's hand or pat him warmly on the back.

If ever there had been any doubt about Duke's hitting power, there was none now. It was clear that Brooklyn had, at last, found the source of extra batting power to make future pennants that much easier. And it was also clear that Babe Herman's all-time Brooklyn record of thirty-five homers set in 1930 would not stand for long.

Gradually the tension grew and was magnified as the fans realized that Snider would have another turn at bat. The undercurrent swelled as fans whispered to one another—could Duke turn the trick again, four homers in four times at bat! In all the history of baseball, it had only been done three times in a nine-inning game: Bobby Lowe in 1894, Ed Delahanty in 1896 and the great Lou Gehrig in 1932.

Never had Duke known greater pressure. As he sat in the dugout, he could almost read his teammates' thoughts: Say nothing. Don't upset him. Maybe he can do it.

Branch Rickey came over, stood a moment looking down proudly at him, then said quietly: "Musial never did it."

Finally, in the seventh inning, it was Duke's fourth turn to come to bat. On the mound, Bob Miller had taken over for Philadelphia. Miller caught the sign and began his windup. Duke stood ready as a nervous quiet settled over Ebbets Field.

Miller threw and Duke connected. The ball, the hardest Duke had hit all afternoon, ripped over the infield like a shot from a cannon, blazing toward the left-center screen. The sphere was rising, but it did not rise quite

[83]

high enough. The ball hit the screen and bounced off with such force that Phillie outfielder Dick Whitman had it in his hands the next moment and on its way back to the infield. As Duke held at first, a great groan went up in the stands. The single had missed being a homer by just four short feet. Then, the 34,000 fans broke into resounding applause, acknowledging Duke Snider as the latest, and perhaps one of the greatest, Dodger stars.

That night, the headlines told the victory story: "DUKE HITS 3 AS DODGERS SWEEP," "HOME RUN SPREE MARKS SNIDER SUCCESS." Sports writer Dick Young of the New York *Daily News* promptly labeled Duke "the triple-threat homer-hitter," and declared that "sudden confidence" had lifted Snider to stardom.

Nothing was said about the years of anguish, of self-doubt, and Duke mentioned this to his roommate Carl Erskine as they read the story together.

"What're you complaining about?" Erskine asked with a smile.

"Not a thing," Duke grinned back. "Let 'em say anything they want. I've arrived and I'm happy to be here!"

Two weeks later, he became the permanent number three man in the Dodger line-up—even when facing left-handed pitching.

The confidence shown in Snider promptly paid off. At midseason he was hitting both right- and left-handed pitchers with equal ease.

In July the fans showed their approval of Duke Snider by selecting him to play in the All-Star game. With him to Chicago went Campanella, Hodges, Newcombe, Reese, Robinson and Preacher Roe. Shotton was to manage the National League team. With all that Brooklyn power, though Duke failed to get a hit in his only trip to the plate as a pinch hitter, the Nationals won it, 4–3, in fourteen innings.

By the middle of August, Duke was batting .310, eighteen points higher than the mark he had posted the previous year.

"Don't press," Erskine said by way of a friendly warning.

"Don't worry," Duke replied with confidence, "I'm not as anxious as I used to be."

Erskine nodded. Fellow outfielder Gene Hermanski, standing nearby, smiled in agreement. "You're right. You even *look* different. You could always hit but you worried yourself to death."

Duke knew that Hermanski's observation was correct. He *was* a great worrier, but this was one year he had nothing to worry about. Rounding out Brooklyn's final western trip, Duke belted three hits in Chicago, two of them doubles, and brought back to Brooklyn a .318 average and a seventeen-game hitting streak.

Nineteen-fifty was Duke's year, but not the year for the Dodgers. The Philadelphia "Whiz Kids" battled Brooklyn right down to the wire, taking the final game to win the pennant.

The bitterness of defeat in Flatbush was sweetened by Duke Snider's brilliant performance for the season. He led the league in hits with 199, belted 31 home runs and finished with a .321 average! He had kept that winter promise to Rickey to justify a $5,000 raise in pay.

8

That winter in Lynwood, California, where Duke and Beverly now made their home, was quiet and uneventful. For once, Duke could relax in the comforting thought that he had finally hit his stride.

He spent most of his time enjoying the pleasures of home and the antics of his son and heir. To keep in condition, he played golf and helped to coach the high school baseball team.

Duke was the local hero, and the boys listened when he made a suggestion. They knew his average, how many home runs he had hit. And he enjoyed basking in the glow of their youthful enthusiasm. He would have been less than human if he didn't admit it.

There was always some youngster wearing a baseball cap who would shuffle up with a pencil and a piece of paper and mumble: "Mr. Snider, can I please have your autograph?"

Duke never said no. As for the coming '51 season, he looked forward to it with heightened anticipation. Would the Dodger management show their appreciation for his outstanding 1950 performance? He wondered, but he didn't have long to wait. His 1951 contract brought a raise that put him in the $18,000 bracket, and Duke and Beverly had a special celebration that night.

He headed for Vero Beach confident he could spark his teammates to a pennant. "It's what I hope will be a big year," he told one reporter as he boarded the train for Florida.

Back in Brooklyn, there had been some radical changes in the Flatbush hierarchy. Branch Rickey had sold his interest in the Dodgers and was moving to Pittsburgh to start rebuilding the Pirates. Walter O'Malley was now the president of the Dodger organization. This immediately gave the armchair strategists something new to mull over as they evaluated Brooklyn's chances of winning the 1951 pennant, to say nothing of a World Series crown, which they had failed to capture in five valiant attempts.

The shrewd and wily O'Malley immediately appointed Fresco Thompson and E. J. (Buzzy) Bavasi as his vice presidents. The next burning question was: Who would manage the team? Burt Shotton was definitely out. Would it be Pee Wee Reese? There had been talk the previous season that if the aging Shotton stepped down Pee Wee would get the nod.

The rumors continued until O'Malley finally made his announcement: "Charlie Dressen will manage the Dodgers in 1951." Most of the baseball fraternity criticized the move, feeling that the popular, hard-working Reese had been bypassed.

"O'Malley should have given the job to you," Duke said to Reese.

But the affable Dodger shortstop took O'Malley off the hook. "You can't play and manage at the same time. At least I can't. I'd rather keep playing. I've got three more good years. After that I'll start thinking about what to do."

Thus, the die had been cast and one of the most incredible seasons in baseball got under way.

For both Duke and the Dodgers 1951 started slowly and quietly with everyone confident Brooklyn would be a shoo-in for the pennant. The stories from Vero Beach hailed Snider as "the greatest potential in the National League" and quoted Dressen as saying he would "bring Snider along for that one step to anticipated greatness."

The first sour note came during an exhibition game at Asheville, North Carolina. Jackie Robinson questioned a call made by umpire Frank Dascoli. One heated word led to another, and Jackie found himself thrown out. It was a hint, for those with a sixth sense about such things, that an ill wind might be blowing in the direction of Brooklyn.

The more sanguine, however, found less forboding signs to suggest clear, bright days ahead. The Dodgers moved rapidly into first place while their arch rivals, the

Giants, promptly dropped into last with an eleven-game losing streak.

"We can't miss!" the optimists among the faithful claimed.

"It's too much too fast," the cynics stoutly held.

The cynics, as it turned out, were right.

O'Malley and his lieutenants had decided that the Dodgers needed "pennant insurance" plus some World Series depth. On June 14, as the Dodgers led the league by six full games, the Brooklyn president announced a startling Chicago-Brooklyn four-for-four player trade.

No trade aroused as much comment or speculation. The Cubs gave Brooklyn outfielder Andy Pafko, pitcher Johnny Schmitz, catcher Al Walker and second baseman Wayne Terwilliger. Brooklyn gave the Cubs pitcher Joe Hatten, catcher Bruce Edwards, infielder Eddie Miksis and outfielder Gene Hermanski.

The deal was called one of the biggest steals in baseball history. In the opinion of most experts, getting the thirty-year-old Pafko—who had hit .304 and hammered out 36 home runs the previous season—clinched the flag for Brooklyn. The Dodgers appeared to have given little —not a single regular—and gotten much. Had the Cubs actually handed Pafko and the pennant to Brooklyn on a silver platter?

Duke read the story and felt uneasy. "Trade talk" always made a player tense and uncomfortable. Now, Duke had a premonition there was more to the story than reported. And suddenly, he found *he* was it!

The evening papers revealed the sensational topper to

the trade: CHI EXPECTED TO LAND DUKE NEXT SEASON! As part of the deal, according to reliable sources, Duke Snider would be traded to the Cubs for $200,000.

Duke felt sick. Now the Cubs-Dodger trade made sense. Brooklyn had to be giving up something, and it was clear that for a price that something was Duke Snider.

He wiped the cold sweat from his brow and continued to pace about his hotel room. The phone rang. He leaped for it. It was Beverly.

"I just read the story in the papers," she started anxiously. "Is it true?"

"I don't know, Honey, I don't know," he said, fighting to keep the anger out of his voice. "Baseball's a business. They do what they want."

He tried to sound cool and self-contained, but he couldn't fool his wife. Playing for Brooklyn had become a way of life, the fulfillment of a dream, certainly a great deal more than just a good way to earn a living.

Beverly's words of comfort did little to untie the knot of anxiety that pressed into the pit of his stomach. As soon as he hung up, the phone rang again. This time it was O'Malley.

"Before you say anything," the Dodger president quickly announced, "let me tell you that the story in the papers is a pack of lies. Sure, the Cubs want you. So does every other team in the league, but it's no deal. Take my word for it."

Duke did take O'Malley's word and the rumors proved to be unfounded, but the shock to Snider had its repercussions. From that day on, slowly and inexorably, Duke's batting average started downward and never recovered. He had hit eighteen homers the first half of the season; now, in July and August he hit only nine.

In August, Brooklyn led the second-place Giants by thirteen and a half games. No one had any doubt that the Dodgers would be in the World Series. Then on August 12 began the final strange turn of events in this weirdest of baseball seasons.

On that day, pitchers Al Corwin and Larry Jansen of the Giants beat the Phillies in a double-header that started the Giants on a fantastic winning streak. After sixteen straight wins, they were within six games of the league-leading Dodgers. There were four weeks left in the season and, day by day, the Giants, with Leo Durocher in command, drew closer to Brooklyn.

Suddenly, the pressure was on the Dodgers, and it appeared that they might actually blow the pennant in these last remaining days. Brooklyn's lead was cut to two games. Then one. And at Boston on September 27 came the most spectacular rhubarb of this most spectacular of seasons.

In the eighth inning, Boston broke up a 3–3 tie against Brooklyn when Bob Addis scored from third on a slow grounder which Jackie Robinson fielded and threw to Roy Campanella at the plate. Frank Dascoli, the umpire, called Addis safe, and the riot began with the roar of outraged Dodgers storming the plate.

When the dust cleared, Dascoli had thrown Campanella and Coach Cookie Lavagetto out of the game and ordered the entire Brooklyn bench cleared! The Dodgers lost, 4–3, and found themselves only a half game in front of the second-place Giants.

On the last day of the season, the Dodgers and Giants were tied for first place. The thirteen-and-a-half-game lead had vanished into thin air. For this final day, the Dodgers were in Philadelphia, while the Giants pressed their pennant hopes against Boston.

While the Dodgers were still locked in mortal combat against the Phillies, the scoreboard showed the Giant 3–2 victory over the Braves. Now the Dodgers had to win to stay alive for a playoff, but they were behind, 8–5.

Duke's average had dropped to .277, and the harder he pressed, the fewer hits he seemed to get. Somehow, Duke couldn't help feeling that if he snapped out of his slump he could still pull the pennant out of the fire.

Although he didn't have a hand in it, the Dodgers tied the score in the eighth inning. And the score remained tied until the fourteenth inning when Jackie Robinson broke it up with a home run.

The pennant race had ended in a tie. The Dodgers were still alive.

In the playoffs, the Giants took the first game and dropped the second. With the playoff tied at one game apiece, tension was almost too much to bear. It seemed as if the entire country had come to a halt just to await the outcome of the game that would decide the National League title for 1951.

Big Don Newcombe took the mound for the Dodgers,

and at the end of eight and a half innings Brooklyn had a commanding 4–1 lead.

With victory and the pennant only three outs away, Duke took his place in center field as the Giants came to bat for the last time.

Some of the fans were already beginning to file out of the stadium. Even the stanchest Giant supporters didn't have much hope. As they shuffled out of the ball park, Alvin Dark hit a single. A few of them turned back. Then Don Mueller stepped up to the plate, beat out a hit, and suddenly everybody froze.

This had been a season of miracles. Was another about to take place? Newcombe pitched to Irvin and got him to foul out.

"One out, two to go," Duke muttered to himself as the Giant's Whitey Lockman stepped up to the plate. Whitey leveled on a pitch for a double, driving in Alvin Dark and sending Mueller to third. The score was now 4–2, with the tying runs on base.

Duke could feel his stomach churning as Giant fans roared their approval. Chuck Dressen, calling time out, walked to the mound, spoke to Newcombe and his catcher, Campanella, and then waved in Ralph Branca from the bullpen.

With two out and men on second and third, Branca had his work cut out for him. Bobby Thomson at the plate represented the winning run.

Branca pumped and delivered. Thomson watched the ball go by for a called strike. On the next pitch, Thomson swung and connected.

Duke began backpedaling as soon as the ball rose from Thomson's bat, but it went over his head and into the stands. With a home run Bobby Thomson had written "The End" to a fantastic, unbelievable season!

The Dodgers went off to lick their wounds while the Giants took on the Yankees in the World Series. As usual, the Yankees won it, this time in six games.

At long last, Duke could go home and seek the solace of the California sunshine. His mind and body ached from the tensions of the past few months, from a nightmarish slump that had come when rumors had placed a $200,000 price tag on his hide. Other players soon forgot the tough-luck days of 1951, but not Duke Snider.

What worried him most, he finally decided, was left-handed pitching. The notion grew and became fixed in his mind. There was no doubt about it. Left-handed pitchers were still his nemesis.

When Duke mentioned it that winter, Ward Snider shook his head. "It's just something to hang your hat on," his father said. "Just a convenient excuse."

Duke used the standard argument of any left-handed hitter. He could do better against right-handed pitchers. Facing a southpaw on the mound meant the strongest pitches usually broke away from him. And, a left-hander could hide the ball in delivery a fraction of a second longer.

Ward Snider refused to agree with his son, and Duke brought some statistics into the discussion. The record showed he had averaged anywhere from 38 to 111 points lower against southpaws. Didn't that prove the point?

"It proves nothing!" his father insisted. "You're the only regular left-handed batter on the team. Naturally any manager with half a brain isn't going to use left-handed pitchers against a right-handed team like Brooklyn. That means you don't get any practice against southpaws. So you don't do as well. It figures."

Duke refused to admit the logic of his father's argument and took his fears right along with him into the 1952 season.

9

●●●●●●●●●●●●●●●●●●●●●●●●●●●●●●●●●●●●●

With Chuck Dressen still at the helm for Brooklyn and Durocher still leading the Giants, 1952 found the two teams battling for the league lead just as they had done in the last month of the previous season.

During the first two dozen games, Duke managed to connect for only three home runs, well off his usual pace. Thoughts of a slump began to drift through his head more and more often. Then came the night of May 21.

The Dodgers, a full game behind the Giants, were playing host to the Cincinnati Reds in a night game at Ebbets Field. There was a sparse 12,000 fans in the park that night as Cox, the Dodger third baseman, grounded out to open the Brooklyn half of the first inning. Reese followed and sweated out pitcher Ewell Blackwell for a walk.

[97]

Next, Duke came to the plate. Something sports columnist Dick Young had written made him smile. "Duke's hair started turning white when he was seventeen and still in high school, so it couldn't have been the left-handed pitchers in the National League." Duke looked at Blackwell and his smile widened. Nothing to worry about. The Cincinnati hurler was a righthander.

Duke sailed into the first pitch and sent it over the right-field scoreboard, driving Reese in ahead of him. And then, for almost an hour, one Dodger followed another until a record-breaking total of twenty-one batters came to the plate to score fifteen runs on ten hits against four Cincinnati pitchers.

Nothing but sheer exhaustion could stop the Dodgers that night as they went on to blast the Reds 19–1 and take over first place by half a game as the Giants dropped a double-header.

In July at All-Star time, for the third straight year Duke was selected to join the Dodger delegation to Shibe Park where the Nationals won again, as they had the two previous years, this time 3–2 in a five-inning game called because of rain.

The trip to Philadelphia failed to do much good for Duke. His batting average plunged twelve points in twelve games and Dressen dropped him from third to sixth place in the batting order. By mid-August, he was limping along at a snail's pace; his leg suddenly started acting up. Maybe that was his trouble, Duke reasoned. Maybe he needed a rest. Get the pressure off the foot. Duke sat out the game that day as Brooklyn shut out the Phillies 15–0. Though the victory was sweet, Snider's anxiety was bitter medicine for the Dodger hierarchy. They decided that something had to be done.

The Dodgers were leaving for the final western swing of the season, opening against the Reds in Cincinnati. Dressen needed Snider, but not on the bench. Duke had failed to get a hit in his last sixteen trips to the plate.

Unknown to Snider, Dressen and Dodger president Walter O'Malley decided upon a course of action. It was a drastic move, one calculated to have a startling and dramatic impact. Dressen put in a phone call to *New York Journal-American* sports writer Mike Gaven and the stage was set.

The next morning, the *Journal-American* carried an "exclusive story" under Gaven's byline:

Charley Dressen has made the most important decision of his managerial career. He has decided to bench Duke Snider, often called baseball's greatest potential star. Until further notice, Andy Pafko will replace Snider in center with Carl Furillo returning to action in right field and George Shuba alternating with Dick Williams in left.

Obviously the ulterior motive is to light a fire under the speedy and hard-hitting 26-year-old outfielder and remind him that he must supplement his great natural talent with more effort.

By the same token he is reminded, and obviously with Walter O'Malley's consent, that he is subjecting himself to a 25% cut in salary unless his play improves when and if he returns to regular duty.

[99]

Dressen's drastic move also tells other clubs that Snider, still a young man, who led the league in total bases and hits in 1950, when he batted .321, probably will be on the market next year.

The carefully worded story was loaded with threat and innuendo. O'Malley and Dressen were playing for keeps. Both practical psychologists, they knew half measures would only add to their problems with Snider. He had to be pushed off the brink, forced to sink or swim.

Duke was unaware of the newspaper story until Beverly called to read it to him. He was still half asleep, having arrived in Cincinnati late the night before along with the rest of the team. Now, as Beverly read Gaven's story, Duke became wide awake and fighting mad.

"It's a lot of trumped-up newspaper stuff!"

"Whatever happens," Beverly said, trying to sound reassuring, "we'll make out."

"Nothing's going to happen!"

"But if it should . . ."

"It won't!" Knowing Beverly was disturbed only further served to aggravate Duke. "Just wait 'til I get my hands on that reporter!"

"Duke, don't do anything foolish."

"You expect me to sit back and say nothing?" he demanded.

Duke finally managed to get Beverly off the phone. He dressed without shaving and went looking for the *Journal-American* sports writer. He found Gaven having breakfast in the hotel coffee shop.

"Hi, Duke," Gaven said casually as though this were just an ordinary day and he hadn't unleashed the most sensational sports story of the season. "Sit down. Have a cup of coffee."

Duke wanted to grab Gaven by the shirt front and give him the shaking of his life, but Beverly's fright kept him from doing anything rash. However, he couldn't keep the anger out of his voice. "Where did you get that 'exclusive' you printed?"

Gaven poured a teaspoon of sugar into his coffee and began to stir it.

"You heard me! Who were you talking to? If I'm going to be traded, *I* want to know about it first."

"I didn't say you were going to be traded," Gaven replied calmly. "I said it *might* happen. *Anything* might happen."

"Don't be a wise guy," Duke roared. "Sure anything *might* happen. I might haul off and sock you. Then you'd really have something to write about!"

"Now, look, Duke, you *are* being benched. If you don't believe me go talk to Charlie Dressen."

"Did he say I was being traded?"

"Why not ask him!" Gaven went back to stirring his coffee and Duke walked off.

"Sure I talked to Gaven," Manager Chuck Dressen said evasively to the livid Duke standing before him. "And yes your name did come up."

"Did you tell him I could be had by the highest bidder?"

"Duke, you know only Mr. O'Malley makes those kind of decisions."

"Well, Gaven must have gotten it somewhere!"

"Duke," Dressen began, then paused to give his words the greatest impact, "it's always a possibility."

"Sure. I know this is a business," Duke snapped. "You'd sell your own father if the price was right. All I ask, when it's my turn, is that you tell me about it before the papers."

Dressen had never seen Snider angrier. And that was good. A *real* fire had been ignited under Duke, so the first step had worked, but would the second? Would he get back in the game and fight so hard he would forget his anxieties?

"Duke, what difference does it make *who* said *what?* The important thing is to forget about guys like Mike Gaven."

"I already forgot about Gaven! What bothers me is being treated like a piece of property in a bargain basement!" Duke stormed out of the room, slamming the door behind him.

That evening, while the Dodgers took on Rogers Hornsby's Reds in a twi-night double-header, Duke Snider warmed the bench. As inning followed inning and he watched his team split the twin bill before the largest night crowd of the season at Crosley Field, Duke sensed a change within himself. The anger he had felt toward Gaven, Dressen and O'Malley he now turned against himself.

Duke knew he alone was to blame for his doubts and

fears. He had distorted his minor failings, his difficulties with left-handed pitchers, completely out of proportion. Ever since childhood, he had tried to be perfect. But he wasn't a perfect human being. No one is.

As he argued with himself, he realized how foolish he had been. This drive for perfection had almost destroyed him. How much better to admit and expect both good and bad days? Then, when the bad ones came along, they didn't throw you. You accepted them as a part of life.

By the time the night game was over, Duke was raring to go. There were six weeks still left in the season. That was time enough to show them, to show *himself,* what he could do. But how to get reinstated gracefully, that was the problem. You just didn't walk up to Chuck Dressen and say, "Give me another chance."

Fortunately for Duke, Walter O'Malley already had prepared "the graceful way out." Quite by accident, the Brooklyn vice president Buzzy Bavasi ran into Duke. In the course of conversation he said, "Mr. O'Malley wants me to assure you he has definitely made no decision about trading you." His instructions were to get Snider back on the playing field—to bring the fire under control, not to put it out.

"What about that twenty-five per cent cut in salary?" Duke asked.

Deliberately avoiding a straight answer, Bavasi said, "Let's see what happens between now and the end of the season."

That was it. Duke could go back to playing ball. The

rest was up to him. It was results they wanted, not excuses.

On Sunday, August 24, the Dodgers moved to St. Louis to take on the red-hot Cardinals who had jumped into second place on the heels of an eight-game winning streak. Some 35,000 fans packed Sportsman's Park, the largest crowd in fifteen years, sensing perhaps something very special in the wind.

Dressen sent his mound ace Preacher Roe against the Cardinals' Cloyd Boyer. In the third inning, Duke leaned into the first pitch and slammed a homer deep into the left-field bleachers. In the sixth he rapped out a single, and followed it with another in the eighth—three straight hits for Duke as the Dodgers wrapped up the ball game, 10–4.

Next day, Brooklyn took both ends of a doubleheader. In the bottom half of the twin bill, Duke hit another homer. With Snider leading the attack, the Dodgers won the next five in a row. Then they returned to Ebbets Field. Duke was home, but the fans had read the story of his benching in the papers. How would they treat him?

Duke had his answer in the third inning of a game against the Giants. Alvin Dark sliced a ball through the infield for a single. The Giants' Whitey Lockman then popped a high fly to right center. Duke moved in quickly, but the wind began playing tricks and sent the ball off to one side. It didn't seem possible for Duke to make the catch, but suddenly he made a side-ways dive with his gloved-hand outstretched, grabbed the ball and held onto it as he went completely over in a somersault! He was still holding the ball when he landed on his feet.

Dark had scampered down to second base, confident that no ordinary human could make such a catch. Now, Duke whipped the ball to Hodges at first for the double play. Giant as well as Dodger fans stamped and shouted their approval. As *Herald Tribune* sports reporter Harold Rosenthal noted: "If Duke's listless play earlier this year had caused him the loss of any rooters, he certainly regained them in a hurry with this one play."

On September 2, the Dodgers blew a double-header, 8–2, 9–3. At the end of the first week in September, the Giants had narrowed the Dodgers' lead to six games from what had been considered an unassailable ten-and-a-half-game lead. It began to look as if 1952 might be a repetition of the disastrous 1951 season.

On September 6, with a high wind over the Polo Grounds which blew the Dodgers no good, the Giants took both ends of a double-header, 6–4 and 7–3, and a mighty groan went up among the Flatbush faithful. They were certain history was about to repeat itself. One of the New York newspapers told the story in black, ominous headlines: THE DODGERS ARE IN TROUBLE.

The Dodgers, with the Giants hot at their heels, had committed four errors in a single game, and by such stalwarts as Reese, Cox, Furillo and Hodges. There was reason indeed for the fans to be concerned.

Though the Dodgers staggered in the final days of the pennant race, the new Duke Snider continued his winning ways. By September 8, he had climbed back up among the ten leading hitters in the National League.

On September 10, Duke averted disaster almost single-handedly by turning the tide in a double victory over the Cubs, 4–1 and 6–2. Duke stepped up to the plate in the first inning of the first game, with bases loaded, to rap out a sharp single and drive in two runs. In the third inning, with a man on first, a third run scored on his resounding triple.

As one reporter put it, "The mourning in Brooklyn stopped abruptly." But there were still precarious days ahead. On September 11, with only fifteen games left in the season, the difference between the Dodgers and Giants narrowed to three and a half games.

Duke, however, was still in there fighting. On the twelfth, in an 8–5 victory over the Cardinals, he belted four singles in five trips to the plate. His batting average had climbed to the .300 mark, seventh highest among the National League's sluggers.

Saturday, the thirteenth, turned out to be as black as any Friday the thirteenth. Brooklyn dropped a 5–2 ball game to St. Louis. Now, the Giants were three games behind.

On Monday, the fifteenth, the Cincinnati Reds moved into Ebbets Field. In the smashing 11–5 Dodger victory, Duke unleashed two homers and a single. Catching his enthusiasm, Robinson homered twice and Hodges once.

Against the Pirates the following night, Duke homered again, clearing the right-field fence by a wide margin, in a 4–2 win. But each Dodger victory was followed by a

Giant win, and the margin between the two teams remained a slim three games until Sunday, September 21.

On that day, Dodger rookie Joe Black held the Braves to three hits giving Brooklyn a vital 8–2 win, while the Phillies beat the Giants 6–2. The combination Dodger win and Giant loss now assured Brooklyn of at least a tie for the pennant.

"The age of miracles," one reporter noted, "would seem to be at an end. With six games left in the season, the Dodgers need but one win to clinch the National League crown."

On the night of September 24 at Ebbets Field, there was desperation in the hearts of Dodger fans as Brooklyn came to bat in the fifth trailing Philadelphia 4–2.

Hodges opened the inning with a looping single to left. Then, Rutherford beat out a sacrifice bunt and there were two on. Cox stepped into the batter's box and dropped a bunt. The Phillies' pitcher, Karl Drews, snagged the ball and whipped it to third forcing Hodges.

Pee Wee Reese was next, with Duke on deck. The fans had already started their rhythmic applause—hoping, praying for a rally.

"Come on, Pee Wee!" Duke called along with a thousand fans as Drews hurled one toward the plate. Reese swung and slashed a line drive off the pitcher's glove which rolled out into center field, sending Rutherford around to score and moving Cox to second. Now it was a 4–3 ball game.

Duke stooped to pick up a handful of dirt and rub it

between his fingers, then tested his grip on the bat and stepped into the batter's box.

Drews pumped and delivered. It was a sinker. Duke lashed out to meet the ball and sent a line drive to right center that rattled off the fence for a double. Cox raced home followed by Reese. Snider had driven across the winning runs, giving the Dodgers their sixth National League pennant in modern baseball history. The Brooklyn fans went wild. What they had anticipated for "next year" had happened here and now!

In the clubhouse as flash guns popped, Duke was smothered by his teammates. Proudly Chuck Dressen and Walter O'Malley posed with their star performer. Every man on the team knew that the final surge to pennant victory would have been impossible without Snider's outstanding performance. That night, the entire Dodger team gathered at the Lexington Hotel to celebrate Walter O'Malley's first victory as Dodger president.

During the festivities, while Duke was busy elsewhere, O'Malley walked over to *Journal-American* reporter Mike Gaven. The two conspirators exchanged a smile. "Well, Mike," O'Malley said, "I think you won the pennant for us. Your story on Snider sure lighted a fire."

"Happy to do it," Mike grinned. "Always been a Dodger fan."

While the Dodgers celebrated at the Lexington, the faithful began lining up in the rain to be first to buy their World Series tickets. The Yankees had clinched the American League pennant for the fourth straight year. This was to be a Subway Series.

When the jubilant O'Malley heard that Dodger rooters were already on line waiting for the ticket offices to
open in the morning, he ordered free coffee and dough-
nuts passed out to all. Never had the Brooklyn management been more magnanimous nor the fans more eager
for the start of a World Series.

10

●●●●●●●●●●●●●●●●●●●●●●●●●●●●●●●●●

Duke approached the '52 series free in mind and spirit. Even the thought of facing Allie Reynolds, who had struck him out three times in a row in the '49 series, didn't bother him.

At exactly 1:00 P.M. on Wednesday, October 1, with the largest crowd ever to witness a World Series game in Ebbets Field packed into the stands, the Yankee-Dodger battle got under way.

With the Yankees favored to win the series, Chuck Dressen had decided to gamble on opening day with his big rookie pitcher Joe Black. For the twenty-eight-year-old right-hander, this would be his third major league start. The Dodgers needed encouragement, and a win behind a freshman pitcher might just do the trick. It was a calculated risk taken by a wily strategist.

Black held the Yankees scoreless in the first inning, and Allie Reynolds followed suit.

In the second, Jackie Robinson's homer put the Dodgers in the lead, 1–0, but Gil McDougald came back in the third with a Yankee blast to tie the score. In the fourth inning, Duke's double off the right-field wall was wasted as his teammates failed to get him home.

With the fans hanging on each pitch, the game remained deadlocked until the Dodger half of the sixth. With two out, Dodger captain Pee Wee Reese singled to right. That brought Duke to the batter's box, and the fans clamoring for action. Reynolds served two bad pitches, hoping to make Snider bite. Duke smiled. By now he had learned to avoid the bad ones. If Reynolds wanted him to swing, he'd have to come up with a good pitch. The next pitch was a called strike. Now, with the count two-and-one, Duke swung on a high curve ball. The crowd rose screaming as the tremendous clout sailed over the right-field scoreboard clock. As he raced around the bases, all Duke could think about was that he had finally settled an old account with Allie Reynolds.

Duke's homer put the Dodgers ahead, and they went on to take the game, 4–2.

Duke was the big hero. Next morning *The New York Times* ran a story under Duke's own byline telling how he had evened up matters with Reynolds. Writing about the vagaries of the game, Duke observed: "You know, they say you're a bum one day in baseball and a hero the next. Now, I know what they mean."

In the second game, Vic Raschi held the Dodgers to

three scattered hits, and the Yankees tied the series with a 7–1 win. The Dodgers went ahead in the third on Preacher Roe's masterful 5–3 victory. But the next day, the Yankees tied it all up with a 2–0 win as Allie Reynolds turned the tables on Joe Black.

Game number five, a Sunday contest, opened beneath a warm, sunny, cloudless sky in Yankee Stadium. Ewell Blackwell was handling the mound chores for the Yankees with Carl Erskine set to do the same for Brooklyn.

In the fifth inning, with a man on, Duke slashed out his second homer, joining Reese as the one other Dodger with two World Series home runs. Brooklyn had developed a comfortable 4–0 lead only to see it chopped down at the hands of that thirty-nine-year-old Yankee stalwart Johnny Mize, who started things off with a three-run homer.

By the seventh, the Yankees had edged ahead 5–4. Duke came to bat with Cox on base, and promptly drove the ball into the outfield scoring Cox and tying up the game again. At 5–5, the game remained deadlocked through the eighth, ninth and tenth innings. In the tenth, the lights were turned on, and the fans prepared to stay through the night if necessary.

The Yankees failed to score in the bottom of the tenth, and that brought the Dodgers to bat with Johnny Sain now pitching against them. Carl Erskine was scheduled to bat first, and Brooklyn manager Dressen decided to let him hit rather than send up a pinch hitter and lose the powerful right-hander in subsequent innings. Erskine struck out. Cox followed with a single into left field, placing the game-winning run on base. And that, as every shouting, screaming, pleading Dodger fan in the park knew, put the game squarely in the hands of Duke Snider.

Sain fired a low curve toward the plate, then tried a change-of-pace, and the Duke connected in royal style. The hard-hit ball sailed over Hank Bauer's head in right field and caromed off the bleacher wall. Duke pulled up at second as Cox raced home with the tie-breaking run. Madness broke loose in the stadium as the Yankees failed to mount an attack in the bottom of the eleventh. With four runs batted in for the day, Duke Snider had given the Dodgers one of the most suspenseful victories in their event-filled history.

The following morning's edition of *The New York Times* found Duke telling, under his own byline, how it felt to be a "King For A Day":

> I always have pretty good luck batting against Johnny Sain but this time I hit the jackpot. . . . Boy, I'm still excited. It's like somebody made me king for a day. . . .
>
> Funny, how sometimes you can start off bad and end up in a bed of roses. . . . I thought I was going to have a real tough day. . . . How much of this excitement can a guy stand?

The strain was far from over, even with the Dodgers leading in the series three games to two. But Duke was taking it all in stride; the pressure was there, but the worry was gone.

Now, the action shifted back to Ebbets Field.

Into the sixth inning neither side had scored when Duke—now hailed as "Brooklyn's mighty siege gun"—stepped up to bat. He took Vic Raschi's first pitch and smashed it over the screening atop the right-field barrier. The ball landed beyond the stadium out on Bedford Avenue. Duke had drawn first blood. Then came the Yankee attack. Berra drove one into the stands to tie the score. Then a second run crossed the plate, and Mantle followed it with still another homer, making it a 3–1 ball game.

In the eighth, Duke sent another Raschi pitch screaming over the right-field fence. It seemed to be Snider against the Yankees. The homer made it 3–2, and that was the way the game ended. But for Snider there was sweetness even in defeat. With four home runs in a World Series, he had tied a record held only by Babe Ruth and Lou Gehrig.

As for the Yankees, they went on to take the last game, 4–2, and the Series.

There was bitter frustration among those whom *New York Times* columnist Meyer Berger had once labeled "the faithful, the feverish and the fanatic." But the Brooks themselves needed no apology for their performance against the Yankees. As for Duke, they called him "magnificent" and "brilliant." He had established two new Series records: most extra bases, 15; most total bases, 24. He had tied four more: most runs batted in, 8; most home runs, 4; most long hits, 6; and two home runs in a single game.

There could be no doubt that the years of trial and error on the part of both the Dodger management and Duke himself had finally borne fruit. The 1952 World Series, as the usually conservative *New York Times* observed, became Snider's "springboard to brilliant stardom."

11

●●●●●●●●●●●●●●●●●●●●●●●●●●●●●●●

Duke's '52 season and Series had made him a star. Hopefully, he could now look forward to adding new and more spectacular laurels to his already-illustrious name.

For the Dodgers, '53 opened slowly. During the first few months of the season, the Flock teetered on the brink of the second division. The Braves moved out in front. Then, gradually, Dodger power began to tell. The "Bums" battled up from fourth to second place, and by the end of June, they were trailing the league leaders by just two slim games. Dodger pitching, however, was weak. Only Carl Erskine could be counted upon to deliver consistently. The sluggers would have to pave the way to the league title if Brooklyn was to win it.

By All-Star time in July, the Dodgers had edged out

in front of the Braves. On July 14, both leagues paused
for the annual battle of stars, originally dreamed up back
in 1933 by Arch Ward, sports editor of *The Chicago
Tribune,* for Chicago's Century of Progress Exposition.

For the fourth straight year Duke was selected to play.
The '53 contest at Crosley Field in Cincinnati seemed
purely a Dodger vs. American League battle. In addition to Snider, the Nationals had Campanella, Furillo,
Hodges, Reese and Robinson. Power at the plate gave
the National League its fourth straight victory, 5–1, and
sent the slugging Dodgers back home on a real tear.
They won sixteen victories in nineteen games, breaking
the pennant race wide open. From the All-Star recess until September, the Dodgers set an incredible pace playing
.820 ball. And on September 12, with Erskine beating
the Braves 5–2, Brooklyn captured their second straight
pennant.

Duke led the league in two departments: total bases
with 370 and runs scored with 132.

Most experts considered the '53 Dodgers the best
Brooklyn team in history. Furillo with a .344 average
was the National League batting champion. Snider
wound up with .336, Robinson had a .329 average, Campanella .312 and Gil Hodges .302.

In addition, the Dodgers had Junior Gilliam, the
Rookie of the Year, at second base. And yet they were
unable to beat the Yankees in the World Series. Setting
a new mark, the Yankees won the crown for the fifth
straight time. They took it in six games, led by Billy

Martin, a .257 hitter during the regular season, who broke loose with a fantastic .500 streak in the Series.

By way of consolation, in addition to the $6,178.42 in each losing player's share, the Dodgers set numerous slugging marks, batting .300, the highest ever for a losing club.

Carl Erskine established a new World Series strike-out record, fanning 14 in the third game to break Howard Ehmke's old record of 13 against the Cubs in 1929. As for Duke, he hit .320 and added one more World Series home run to his record. But when all was said and done, the Dodgers still couldn't lick the Yankees. It had been their fourth try and their fourth failure.

With no progress being made in World Series competition, Walter O'Malley refused to give Chuck Dressen, who demanded a three-year guarantee, more than a one-year contract to continue managing the team. Durocher and other Brooklyn managers had received longer contracts when the team hadn't done nearly as well, Dressen argued. But O'Malley refused to yield. It was a one-year deal, take it or leave it! Dressen left it, and Brooklyn was suddenly without a manager.

When Duke heard the news, he thought immediately that the thirty-four-year-old Pee Wee Reese would finally be given the managerial post he so richly deserved. The Dodger brass kept everyone guessing, then made the announcement: Walter Alston would manage the Flock in '54.

In the meanwhile, Duke turned from baseball to devote time and energy to his family, luxuriating in the mild California winter weather, and enjoying the newest member of the Snider household, a daughter named Pamela. He passed an occasional evening with Beverly and friends playing bridge. One such card game was destined to change his life.

It was a warm evening. After an hour of bridge, Duke left the card table to stretch his legs. He walked to the big picture window overlooking Cliff Dapper's two and a half acres of avocado trees and remembered the conversation he had had with Cliff in a Montreal hospital years ago.

"You know," Duke said to Cliff, "I still wouldn't mind owning a few of those trees myself someday."

Beverly smiled. "Duke's really a farmer at heart."

"Oh, I don't know how much of a farmer I am," Duke said. "But I sure get a thrill seeing things grow."

Cliff noted the earnestness with which his friend spoke. "You really interested?"

"Sure. Nothing big. Just something on a small scale. Everybody's got a hobby. What's wrong with avocados?"

"Nothing." Cliff thought a moment, then grinned. "You got time to take a drive tomorrow?"

"Where to?"

"A town called Bonsall down in San Diego County."

"What's there?"

"Avocados."

"So?"

"You'll see. I'll pick you up at nine in the morning."

Cliff handled the car easily as they drove along the winding road from Bonsall toward the inland avocado and citrus country. It was the first time Duke had seen ranch country up close, and he was thrilled by it.

"What makes you think this guy will sell his land?" Duke asked.

"He's a baseball fan."

"So are a lot of people, but that doesn't mean they'll give up the land they own."

"This man is a particular fan of some joker named Duke Snider."

Duke couldn't help laughing. "You using my reputation to promote some crooked deal?"

"Look, Duke, there's nothing crooked about it. This Bill Shaw has sixty choice acres . . ."

"Sixty acres! I don't need a business. All I want is a hobby."

"I'll take half."

"That still leaves me with thirty acres! What am I going to do with all that land?"

"Grow avocados!"

Duke grumbled some more, then asked, "How much does he want?"

"Don't inject crass commercialism. Just talk to Mr. Shaw about baseball, and how maybe *next* year the Dodgers might win the World Series."

There was nothing Bill Shaw enjoyed more than baseball talk. And Cliff had no trouble keeping the conversation away from business until Shaw was thoroughly impressed with Duke Snider, the Dodger baseball star. As for Duke, he looked across the gently sloping land, liked what he saw, and allowed Cliff to manage the details. The afternoon sun had begun to settle behind the distant hills when Cliff got down to serious trading.

"What I've been telling Duke," he said, "is invest your money. It won't always be big ball parks and World Series paychecks."

"Yes, sir!" Shaw agreed. "Land is what you want to turn your money to. Ever thought of buying property down this way?"

When the trading and talking was over, Duke and Cliff had bought Bill Shaw's sixty acres at slightly over $400 an acre. It was a $27,000 deal which the two friends split down the middle, with Dapper taking the thirty acres to the east.

That winter Duke and Beverly spent most of the time talking about their "ranch." At first, the idea of raising "some avocados" had been looked upon as a pastime. But now that the Snider family owned a full thirty acres, Duke suddenly saw an opportunity to get close to the soil and build, literally from the ground up—first a home they would design themselves, then learn to handle a tractor, level the land, and turn the soil.

Spring training was only two months away and Duke felt on top of the world. The land he now owned, the vision of what it could mean for his family, the security it might bring when he played his last ball game, all this gave him a sense of well-being, a sense of both direction and purpose.

Then, in February, Duke opened a copy of *The Saturday Evening Post* to find himself the subject of a scathing feature article entitled, "The Dodgers' Problem Child." According to writer Arthur Mann, Duke Snider was that "problem child." Headlined across the top of the article in bold, black letters was this quote:

"It's really not my fault," pleaded Duke Snider when he was ordered out of a training camp for not hustling. "My parents are to blame. I'm an only child."

Trembling with rage, Duke read through the remainder of the story. He had never uttered an unkind word about his mother or father in his life. Here he was, thrust before the public, made to appear a petulant young man not terribly concerned with the welfare of his team and unhappy over the chafing of Dodger discipline.

Duke wanted to sue, but Beverly pleaded with him to overlook the "jazzed-up" publicity. If he made a fuss, it would only call more attention to the negative aspects of the article. There was really nothing to be gained; the damage had already been done.

"Just make up your mind that one day you'll tell your own story in your own words," Beverly said wisely.

Duke knew she was right. If he permitted his anger to flare out of control, he would only add fuel to the fire. Duke wasn't the type to feel that *any* publicity is good publicity; he preferred to be left alone. He hated the notoriety, but there was no place to hide.

As the 1954 season started, Duke tried to ignore the reporters and the sports writers, but Snider was news.

Most of them had little interest in the supposed "revelations" in *The Saturday Evening Post*. They were more concerned with comparing Duke Snider to the Giants' pride and joy, Willie Mays, the twenty-two-year-old slugging sensation from Birmingham, Alabama, who had joined the Giants in 1951. Who was the greater star, Snider or Mays?

Duke tried to avoid such discussions, but comparisons make good newspaper copy, and the reporters continued to hound him.

"The way Mays is going is good for baseball," Duke admitted to sports columnist Jimmy Cannon one afternoon.

"Doesn't it appeal to your professional pride?" Cannon wanted to know.

"I'd like to do everything better than he," Duke replied. "We're in this game to win pennants and make money. But I don't feel I'm in a contest with him. I don't pick up the paper every day to see how Mays is doing."

When Cannon asked Snider's opinion of the Giant outfielder, Duke admitted Mays' tricky catch had "too much show in it." He took all fly balls with his hands held belt high, the cupped palms forming a cradle. Then Duke grinned and added: "But he does all right with it, doesn't he? So there you are."

Duke figured he was being paid to play ball, not grant interviews, and confined himself to the business at hand. But there were problems. Walter Alston, the new Dodger manager, had inherited a dugout full of troubles. Age had caught up with Jackie Robinson and Billy

Cox. Campanella sustained a hand injury which crippled his sorely needed batting punch, and Carl Furillo, the batting champ of '53, went into a slump.

In the pitching department, joining Carl Erskine and Preacher Roe on the mound for the Dodgers, were Don Newcombe, just back from the Army, Billy Loes, Clem Labine and Russ Meyer. In addition, there was Johnny Podres who had won nine for the Dodgers in his rookie season the previous year. Podres suddenly became an appendicitis victim.

They were calling Brooklyn "the lackluster Dodgers of 1954." Most of the blame was heaped on Manager Alston, who had never coached or managed in the major leagues before. The Dodgers, some fans said, had more flash and fire under Dressen. Now they were playing conservative, cautious ball. Alston, other critics claimed, coddled his players, did not push them to maximum effort, despite aches, pain and age. The only member of the team who didn't seem to lack the old flash was Duke Snider, and the Decoration Day battle against the Phillies gave him a chance to prove it.

The game had gone into extra innings and, at the bottom of the tenth, the Dodgers nursed a one-run lead. The Phillies were at bat with two out, the winning run on first and the tying run on second. As third baseman Willie Jones came to bat, the Philadelphia fans began clamoring for a hit.

The first pitch to Jones was inside and low; the next was a high and hard one. Both were balls. Jones sensed the next one would be good. It was and he swung on it.

The fans came up with a roar as they followed the ball to deep left center. It looked like a home run.

With the crack of the bat, Duke had turned from the plate and dashed toward the wall. Then, he leaped, dug his spikes into the wall, boosted himself up and backhanded the ball. He hit the wall with a thud and came back down to the ground on his knees.

Duke rose painfully from the ground to thunderous applause for his courage. He had made a magnificent save to end the game and give the Dodgers the victory. The experts called it one of the greatest catches in baseball history.

The next day, a reporter asked Giant Manager Leo Durocher to comment on Snider's fabulous catch. Could Mays match it?

"It was a very good catch," Durocher acknowledged flatly.

"Have you ever seen a better one?" a reporter asked.

Durocher laughed. "You're expecting me to tell you Mays had one that was better. Well I won't." And then Leo added: "But I think Duke did. It was one he made at Yankee Stadium in the '52 Series. He had to run into right center and worry about the wall. He could've killed himself."

To match his superb fielding, Duke continued to blast opposing pitchers at the plate. In the All-Star game in July, at Municipal Stadium, Cleveland, Duke collected three hits and drove in two runs in four trips to the plate. Unfortunately, it didn't bring the Nationals their fifth win in a row. In 1955 the Americans took the annual classic, 11–9, behind the managerial skills of Casey Stengel.

Throughout the season, the pennant race had been the now-annual duel between Brooklyn and the Giants. But as the final month approached, interest centered for National League fans on still another battle: the batting championship.

With a torrid .342 average, Duke was on top for the crown. Hot on his heels, a fraction of a percentage point behind, stood Willie Mays and his Giant teammate Don Mueller.

The final week of the season brought the showdown series between the Dodgers and the Giants. The Giants took the first of three games, 7–1, to clinch the pennant. But the question of who would emerge National League batting champion of the year was far from settled.

With three hits in the Giant victory, Mays moved four percentage points ahead of Duke, and five ahead of Mueller. But by the last day of the season, Duke, Mays and Mueller were so close together again it took a fourth decimal place to separate them. Mueller led with .3426, Duke followed with .3425 and Mays trailed with .3422.

On the last day, Duke went hitless against Jack Thies of the Pirates. Against Robin Roberts of the Phillies, Mays collected three hits and a walk; Mueller beat out a hit. The final order stood: Mays, .345, Mueller, .342, Snider, .341.

Although he missed taking the batting crown, Duke led the league for the second year in slugging percentage with a .647, and tied for runs scored with 120. And for his sensational wall-climbing catch in Philadelphia, Duke received the Dell Award for the 1954 catch-of-the-year.

Duke had accurately predicted coming events when he told sports reporter Mike Gaven earlier in the season: "This could be a big year for me."

It turned out to be the best ever. And Duke, who had not permitted the adverse publicity nor the reporters' questions to disturb him, was handsomely rewarded. From now on he would receive nominal yearly raises. There would be no cuts. There would be no arguments. With his raise for the 1955 season, Duke moved into the $40,000 class. At twenty-seven, the youngest Dodger regular wasn't doing badly!

12

●●●●●●●●●●●●●●●●●●●●●●●●●●●●●●●●

The gloom that had settled over Manager Walt Alston at the end of the previous season lifted in the first days of the 1955 campaign. The Dodgers won ten in a row.

During game number two, in a gloomy setting of rain and mud, Duke added still another touch of brilliance to his career. It was a 10–8 slugfest, with the Dodgers out in front when the Giants' Monte Irvin stepped to the plate in the ninth inning with two out and men on first and second. Irvin, at the plate, represented the winning run.

On a fast ball from Jim Hughes, Irvin sent a line drive screaming deep to the outfield, slightly to Snider's left. It looked like a lost cause, but Duke turned and, with his back to the plate, raced toward the wall. At the last moment, he spun around, jumped, backhanded the ball, fell, rolled over, and then came up with the ball in his hand to show he had made a fair catch! The Polo Grounds spectators stomped and shouted themselves hoarse. The Dodgers had won it in spectacular Snider fashion.

In the dressing room after the game, a reporter asked Duke how he thought his catch compared to a similar one Mays had made during the '54 Series.

"I only saw his on TV," Duke replied. "What made his so good was that he caught the ball over his shoulder. But from what I saw, he caught his on the grass. I caught mine on the cinders. I was only about four feet from the wall when I grabbed it."

At that point, Campanella joined the discussion. "I saw both catches. Duke's and Mays'. Duke ran as far as he could and jumped as high as he could, and he still came up with the ball. What more can a man do?"

"He can run into a wall," Duke said seriously. "I think the one I made in Philadelphia last year was the best catch I ever made."

Although Duke didn't have the flamboyance of Willie Mays or the flashing speed of Mickey Mantle, the sports analysts began to compare him to the great Joe DiMaggio. "Snider goes about his business quietly," Joe Sheehan noted in *The New York Times,* "making the hard chores seem easy. Mickey and Willie have a long way to go before they can put on the record that they measure up to Snider."

When asked his opinion of Duke, Manager Walt Alston responded, "Let's just say that it's nice to have a guy like that on your side every day."

Alston's comment proved to be the understatement of 1955.

Duke's booming bat could be heard in every National League ball park. On April 15, he slammed out a towering three-run 460-foot homer in a 6–3 victory over the Giants. Three days later, he belted another three-run homer in a 5–2 win over the Phillies. Three days more, and Duke walloped still another three-run homer in a 14–4 rout of the Phillies. On May 1, Duke drove one out of the ball park that accounted for two runs in a 5–4 conquest of the Braves.

The Brooklyn outfielder had suddenly created a reign of terror among rival pitchers, and fans began to talk about the possibility of his winning batting's triple crown. No National Leaguer since Joe Medwick in 1937 had won the batting, home-run and runs-batted-in title in the same season.

In the first fifty games of the year, Duke failed only once to reach base on a hit or a walk. On May 4, he was back to his home run campaign. His blow that day gave the Dodgers an easy 12–4 victory over the Cardinals. Then on May 8, Duke topped it off with a grand-slam homer that won the game, 9–8, over the Phillies.

Snider's batting spree shot him to the top of the major league home-runs and runs-batted-in standing. His dazzling display at the plate was matched by his brilliance in the outfield. In addition to the great catch of Monte Irvin's long drive on the second day of the season, he brought the fans to their feet with his catch on April 18 in Pittsburgh that robbed Felipe Montemayor of a triple.

Even on the bases, Duke had become a threat. Twice he managed to move from first to third on a sacrifice bunt. In St. Louis on May 5 against the Cards, he did exactly that to set up the winning run, which he then scored.

For the moment at least, there was no one who could equal his performance. When one more reporter laughingly asked, "Who's better, you or Willie Mays?"

Duke grinned and said, "I am. I get paid more."

The anxious yesterdays were gone forever. Instead of worrying about opposing pitchers, Duke now had *them* worried. And with continuing cause. On June 1, against the Braves, Duke slammed out three home runs in a single game! Flatbush went wild. It was the second time in his career that he had accomplished such a feat. Five years earlier, on May 30, 1950, he had bagged three against the Phillies.

During that first week in June, Duke just couldn't be stopped. In fourteen trips to the plate, he collected eleven hits.

Sports columnist Milt Gross, of *The New York Post,* wrapped up the situation succinctly when he said: "There is scarcely anything Snider cannot do better on the ball field than any other man in the game today."

Then suddenly, for no apparent reason, in mid-August Duke went into a slump, going thirteen trips to the plate without a hit. His average dropped from .331 to .299. Duke's plight became the Dodgers' plight.

Without the power of his bat, Brooklyn's twelve-and-a-half game lead over the second-place Braves might evaporate as quickly as their thirteen-and-a-half-game lead had disappeared in 1951.

Frustrated Brooklyn fans, nerves frazzled, were ready to explode. Five times they had thrilled to a pennant without the sweet victory of a World Series title. This season, the Yankees, fighting to hold on to a narrow one-game lead, looked somewhat less than invincible. Here was the year, *if* the Dodgers could hold on. And that meant ultimate victory rested heavily on Duke Snider's shoulders.

On Thursday, August 26, with Cincinnati at Ebbets Field to open a three-game series with a double-header, tension reached the breaking point. In the sixth inning of the first game, with two out and bases loaded, Duke stepped to the plate.

The fans roared their encouragement. Duke tried, but it wasn't good enough. He grounded out and the fans began to boo. It was a Ladies Day crowd of almost 19,000 strong that gave full voice to their frustration.

As he trotted out to center field, something hard nicked his shoulder and fell to the ground. It was a metal beer can opener!

Duke slammed his fist into his glove. He had never been angrier in his life. It's the same old thing, he thought, they love you when you're up and kick you when you're down. Again he pounded his fist against the leather, struggling to control the pent-up rage within him. But he couldn't do a thing at bat, and the Dodgers lost, 8–5.

That night they dropped the other end of the double-header, 6–5. It was the first time such a catastrophe had occurred during the entire season, and the Brooklyn faithful lost heart. Deeply stung by their hostility, Duke announced to the clubhouse reporters after the debacle, "They don't deserve to win a pennant. They're the worst bunch of fans in the league!"

He handed one of the reporters the beer can opener that had been thrown at him. "Maybe we ought to stage a 'Boo Snider Night,' and give away prizes," he said bitterly. "I'll put up a hundred dollars for the loudest and nastiest fan!"

Duke's angry blast received more coverage than the details of the game itself. He had reacted instinctively to the unfair "criticism."

Pee Wee Reese handed Duke the newspaper the next morning with the observation, "You should have kept your mouth shut."

The headline convinced Duke that Pee Wee was right. Big, black letters across the front page announced: "Duke Raps Dodger Fans!"

"For Pete's sake, I was only letting off a little steam. When you're lousy, you know you're lousy, but you don't like to be reminded of it." He handed the paper back to Pee Wee. "They'll probably tear me apart to-night."

When the news reached California, Duke received a phone call from his mother.

She reported that the family was well, then asked him about his clubhouse comments.

"Well, I suppose I shouldn't have popped off that way. But they made me plain mad."

"I thought I had raised a smarter son than that," came the quiet response.

"You did. But I needed to get it off my chest. Maybe the blow-up'll do me some good."

"I hope so, son."

That night, in the third game against the Reds, he collected three hits. The scattered boos were swiftly drowned out by an avalanche of applause.

Duke and the Dodgers, the fans knew, were back to their winning ways. But one thing the fans didn't know: Duke's irritation could be traced back to something that had happened in Chicago earlier in the month.

Sliding into second base, in a game against the Cubs his spikes had caught in Gene Baker's flannels. His left knee was badly wrenched, bringing back the old injury suffered in junior high school. The pain was pure torture, but he refused to give in to it.

He had hit his thirty-eighth home run of the season early in August, placing him seven days up on Babe Ruth's record. But from the time he was hurt in Chicago until the end of the year, he hit only four more homers.

When Duke had cried out against the fans, he had also cried out against the weakness of his own body. The recurrent left-leg injury to a left-handed batter who needs to pivot off his left leg was like asking a one-legged man to run, skip and jump.

Duke finished off the season with a .309, certainly nothing to be ashamed of. He had collected 42 home runs and led the league in runs batted in with 136.

The Dodgers held on to clinch the flag, while the Yankees came through again in the American League. Now, once more it was a Subway Series.

Just prior to opening day of the Series, sports writer Milt Gross summed up Duke Snider in these words: "Here is a great player who wants to be among the great greats and wonders if he'll ever make it."

13

●●

Up in the Bronx, the Yankees were confident. Over in Dodgertown, Brooklyn supporters dreaded a repeat of past Yankee-Dodger encounters.

The press noted Pee Wee Reese's complaint: "I'm the only guy in history who ever played in five World Series without winning one—and all against the same team. How long can it last?"

"I hate those Yankees," one paper quoted a fan as saying. "But what makes me mad is that they'll win anyway."

Even foreign visitors were riding with the favorites. For the first time since the end of World War II, ships of the Japanese Navy were paying an official visit to New York. The captain announced that his sailors, given time off to see a World Series game, were unanimously Yankee fans.

Strongest pre-Series Dodger support came from sports columnist Red Smith of *The New York Herald Tribune:* "The Dodgers in six."

Some 64,000 fans jammed Yankee Stadium on opening day as Yankee ace Whitey Ford took the mound against Brooklyn's Don Newcombe.

As Duke led off for Brooklyn in the third inning, with the score tied, 2–2, he faced the Yankee southpaw without any worries. He worked the count to three-and-two, then sent a waist-high curve ball screaming into the upper right-field deck.

It was Duke's sixth World Series home run, a National League record!

Furillo also homered for the Dodgers, and Jackie Robinson stole home, the ninth player ever to do so in Series history. Despite this, the Yankees took the opener, 6–5.

The second game seemed to prove that the old Yankee-Dodger World Series pattern was unfolding once again. Yankee pitcher Tommy Byrne drove in the winning run himself as Casey Stengel's "invincible team" took it, 4–2.

Yankee victory now appeared certain. No team had ever lost the first two games and come back to win the championship.

As the action shifted to Ebbets Field, one sports observer noted: "Only a blatant Brooklyn optimist can look forward to a pleasant Ebbets Field weekend as we move to Flatbush for the swift conclusion to what has become an inevitable occurrence."

In the Dodger clubhouse, Duke walked across to left-hander Johnny Podres, whom Manager Alston was sending in to pitch game number three. Today was Podres' twenty-third birthday.

Duke said: "Birthdays are always good luck. I have a feeling you'll give us all something to celebrate."

Podres held the Yankees to seven hits, and the Dodgers won, 8–3.

Beneath a dark, gray Saturday afternoon sky, game number four began. For the first three innings, it looked as if the brief moment of victory had ended. The Yankees took a quick 3–1 lead. In the bottom of the fourth, the Dodgers broke loose with homers by Campanella and Hodges plus a single by Furillo sandwiched in between. Now it was 4–3 Brooklyn.

Gilliam drew a base on balls to open the Dodger fifth. Reese followed. Yankee hurler Don Larsen failed to find the plate with the first two pitches to Reese, and Stengel yanked him. In from the bullpen came young Johnny Kucks to pitch his first Series game.

As Kucks faced Reese, Gilliam took a lead off first, started to run with the wind-up and made a clean steal of second base.

Then, Pee Wee rapped a grounder toward Yankee first baseman Joe Collins. Back deep from the bag, Collins fielded the ball and looked for someone to throw to. It should have been Kucks, but he had hesitated before moving to first to catch the relay from Collins. Pee Wee was safe at first on Kucks' fatal fielding error.

The next man up was Duke and now Kucks had to

pitch to him. If Reese had been thrown out, Duke would have been walked to set up a possible double play to end the inning.

When Duke stepped to the plate, he knew the rookie pitcher was rattled and might be replaced at any moment. He had to strike while he could for Kucks' replacement might not be as easy to handle.

Duke swung at the first pitch, a sinking fast ball, and drove it over the fence for a three-run homer that scored Gilliam and Reese in front of him. Home run number two in this Series, his seventh in World Series competition!

The sky may have been dark and gray, but there was sunshine in Brooklyn as the Dodgers took the fourth game, 8–5, to tie the Series at two apiece.

In the fifth game, Manager Alston gambled on rookie pitcher Roger Craig, who had been brought up from Montreal in midseason. It was the type of move that put the forty-three-year-old manager squarely on the spot, a prime target for second-guessers.

"Craig has courage and he doesn't scare," Alston told a reporter. "And he's got a fine assortment of pitches."

The largest crowd ever to watch a game in Ebbets Field packed the ball park to witness Craig's battle against Bob Grim and the Yankees.

What they saw was a record-shattering performance by Duke Snider. In the third and then again in the fifth inning, he slammed the ball out of the park. That gave him a total of four in the Series. In '52, he had equaled the record set by Babe Ruth and Lou Gehrig of four homers in a single Series. Now, he became the first player in history to hit that many in *two* Series!

Duke's handsome, smiling face graced the front pages of newspapers across the country as the press heralded his achievement in the 5–3 Dodger victory. *The New York Times,* in addition to noting that the Dodgers now led in the Series three games to two, pinned the title "Duke of Flatbush" on the Brooklyn hero.

His fantastic power at the plate had captured the imagination of every baseball fan in the nation. Even the irate Casey Stengel shook his head in bewilderment.

"He shouldn't get that many homers," he told a reporter, "after we get two strikes on him. Snider's a streak home-run hitter. He hit forty-two in the regular campaign, none of them after Labor Day. Now he's back in a streak for the Series."

Duke read Casey's statement and hoped the Yankee manager was right. The Dodgers had one more to go to take the championship. He recalled that three years ago, when Brooklyn had also led after five games, they faltered in the last two games at Ebbets Field. This time they would have to play the last game in the wide open spaces of Yankee Stadium, where they had dropped the first two games.

After three straight setbacks, the Bombers staged a five-run attack to open the sixth game as Bill Skowron broke loose with a three-run homer.

In the bottom of the third, Skowron came up to bat again. In center field, Duke set himself and waited as Karl Spooner hurled toward the plate. Skowron swung and lofted an easy fly ball to center. As Duke started after it, his foot caught in a small hole. Something snapped in his left knee and a flash of pain shot through his leg. He recovered in time to catch Skowron's fly ball, then hobbled back to the dugout as the inning ended.

Alston's face showed concern. He had caught the flicker of pain on Snider's face.

"What happened?"

Duke tried to shrug it off. "Just gave it a yank."

Alston wasn't buying that explanation. He remembered Duke's injured knee in Chicago earlier in the season. "Bend your leg," he ordered.

"I'm O.K."

"Bend your leg!" Alston insisted.

Duke tried it, his face showing some of the pain.

"I'm sending Zimmer in for you."

"I'll be all right."

"Not on your life," Alston snapped. "If we lose today, there's always tomorrow. And if you take care of that leg, you might be in shape to do some good."

Duke argued, but the Dodger manager refused to listen. Duke was sent to the clubhouse to give his leg a whirlpool bath and some much-needed rest.

A gasp of surprise swept through the stands in the top of the fourth when Don Zimmer was announced to pinch-hit for Duke.

Whitey Ford held the Dodgers to four scattered hits as the Yankees went on to win, 5–1.

Reporters tried to get in to see Duke. How bad was his injury? Would he be able to play in the final game?

Duke said he would make it if his leg didn't stiffen. The doctor had encased his left knee in an elastic bandage.

The finale at Yankee Stadium on October 4 saw Alston call on Johnny Podres to carry the Brooklyn hopes. Duke was in the game, fighting pain every time he swung at the plate, but refusing to give up. Podres' brilliant shut-out pitching gave the Dodgers a 2–0 victory and their first championship in history.

Pandemonium broke loose in Yankee Stadium. In Brooklyn there was wild delirium. Motorcades raced up and down every major thoroughfare. Cowbells clanged, horns tooted, firecrackers exploded, while people hung out of windows banging on pots and pans.

Walter O'Malley used the Dodger success to demand a new stadium for the champions. Borough President John Cashmore promised to order a survey, and shrugged off any thought that the Dodgers would ever consider recent offers to play outside the borough.

"We'll never leave Brooklyn," Duke told one reporter. "I wouldn't be at home anywhere else." For him, there was trepidation mixed with joy as he looked toward the future. He had hoped for at least five more good years before retiring to avocado ranching. Now, the recurring injuries to his left knee forced him to ask the all-important question: How long could he hope to remain in major league baseball?

14

●●●●●●●●●●●●●●●●●●●●●●●●●●●●●●●●●●●●●●

On January 7, 1956, Duke was voted Player of The Year by the New York Chapter of the Baseball Writers Association of America. Then he was named Major League Player of the Year by *The Sporting News.*

Duke loved the honors heaped upon him, but his future, along with that of all the Dodgers, was very uncertain. There was talk of moving the Dodgers out of Brooklyn.

Baseball was big business and there wasn't enough money in Brooklyn. Also Dodger president Walter O'Malley insisted that the small and ancient Ebbets Field was no fit home for the champions of the world.

Everyone agreed but no one did anything about it. So home games played away from home were O'Malley's way of saying a move from Brooklyn was no idle threat.

Already the Dodgers had played seven homes games in Jersey City.

Public awareness of the business realities of baseball became evident in 1953 with the move of the Boston Braves to Milwaukee, the first major league shift in fifty years. The following year, the St. Louis Browns had been transferred to Baltimore and became known as the Orioles. In 1955, the Philadelphia Athletics went to Kansas City but retained the Athletics' name. Clearly, it could happen to Brooklyn, but the more rabid fans refused to believe O'Malley would desert the shores of the Gowanus Canal.

As for Duke, he preferred not to think about it. He liked Ebbets Field. If any ball park could be a home, this was it. With a game leg he needed the comfort and security of a stadium he knew.

One day, he received a call from an editor at *Collier's* magazine. How would he like to tell his story of what it meant to be a major leaguer? The editor mentioned a sizable sum for the required literary effort.

"What's there to tell?" Duke said. "You spend half your life away from the family, sleep on trains and eat at peculiar hours. Sometimes it can be a nightmare."

"Would you put it in writing?" the editor persisted.

"I'm no writer."

"We'll get you one to work with."

Duke hesitated, then said he would have to consult his wife.

That night he reminded Beverly of her advice when *The Saturday Evening Post* article had come out. "Some-

[144]

day you'll have a chance to tell *your* side of baseball. You said that, remember?"

Beverly nodded.

"Don't you think this is the time?" Duke asked.

"I do," Beverly agreed.

"But no punches pulled. The truth. Whatever I want to say about how I feel." It was a statement rather than a question.

"What do you want to say?" she asked.

Duke paced as he thought, then turned to face his wife. "That it's not all peaches and cream. That I hate the kids who throw skate keys and marbles at my head when I'm backed up close to the stands. That I hate the jokers who toss beer cans off my knees during a dull game. I want to say that there are some sports writers who don't know any more about baseball than my four-year-old daughter."

"Then you've decided," Beverly said with a smile.

"What's that?"

"To write the article."

Duke grinned. "Yeah—there's a lot I want to get off my chest."

"I Play Baseball For Money—Not Fun" was the title finally used by Duke Snider and Roger Kahn in the *Collier's* magazine piece published on May 25, 1956. It created quite a stir.

There were those who declared Duke was destroying the image of our national sport, wrecking the dreams of every youngster playing sandlot ball in America. But most readers recognized the truth and applauded Duke for it. He had leveled with the fans—no phony heroics, just straight-from-the-shoulder talk.

Duke described his great friendship with men like Pee Wee Reese and Carl Erskine. But he also told of having to take sleeping pills in order to catch four and a half hours of sleep on a train and then follow the overnight train ride with an afternoon game. "When you're short of sleep," Duke wrote, "you better bunt and hope."

He wrote about the revelations that come with maturity, when the boyhood fantasies are gone. "The pay is good," Duke admitted, "but they take it out of you in sweat and worry."

Along with the sweat and worry, 1956 had plenty of color and excitement for Duke in a thrilling, tension-packed pennant race between the Dodgers, the Reds and the Braves.

The Dodgers were considered "the old pros," who had the pennant-winning habit, five times in the last nine years. The Reds had one of the most powerful hitting teams ever put together, and the Braves had good power at the plate combined with phenomenal pitching.

One sports expert made a study of just how old "the old pros" really were. Robinson and Reese were thirty-seven; Campanella, thirty-five; Furillo, thirty-four; Hodges, thirty-two; Snider, soon to be thirty.

Brooklyn moved out to an early league lead in April on the heels of a five-game winning streak. Then, they dropped four in a row and plummeted to fourth place. By May, they were in fifth place.

The Dodgers discovered they had more than their share of trouble. Duke's leg was still creating a problem. Podres, the World Series pitching sensation, was in the Navy. Erskine's arm was acting up. Labine wasn't coming through in relief, and rookies Craig and Bessent were both off their 1955 stride. Only Newcombe could be counted on with any consistency to win a ball game. As it turned out, he won twenty-seven for the Dodgers during the season.

In a desperation move, O'Malley made a deal with Cleveland to acquire the aging, onetime great Giant pitching star, Sal "The Barber" Maglie, who had trimmed the Dodgers more than once.

Manager Walt Alston used Newcombe and Maglie one day after another, juggled his line-up, and switched around his infielders and outfielders. To the outsider, Alston seemed a madman hoping for a miracle. But the insiders knew that from the judicious juggling might come just the right combination.

In June the Dodgers began climbing back toward the top. By September there was a wild scramble for first place among Cincinnati, Milwaukee and Brooklyn. On September 15 the Dodgers beat the Cubs, and the Braves lost to the Phillies, putting Brooklyn out in front by two percentage points. The Dodgers held tenaciously to the league lead and never let go.

"The old pros" did it in '56. Again Brooklyn had captured a pennant. Duke's contribution? He emerged the home run king of the National League with 43, led in slugging percentage with .598, was the most frequently walked player with 99 bases on balls, and passed the 100 mark in runs batted in for the sixth time in his career.

The Dodgers moved into the World Series, once more against the Yankees, and this time it looked as if Brooklyn might displace the Yankees as World Champions. The Dodgers took the first two, 6–3 and 13–8. But then, the roof fell in. The Yankees swept three in a row, allowed the Dodgers to tie up the series with a ten-inning 1–0 victory, and then proceeded to trounce Brooklyn 9–0 for the crown. One distinction the Dodgers did have: in the fifth game they became the first victims of a World Series perfect game, pitched by Don Larsen.

The Series tensions over, Duke could scarcely wait to get back to California and see his family, which now numbered four. Seven-year-old Kevin, Duke's firstborn named in honor of Kevin (Chuck) Connors, now had a sister, Pamela, five, and a baby brother, Kurt.

Each fall, Duke came to life in a very special way. The months ahead with his wife and children were the rich reward for the strain and pressure of the baseball season. And now in 1956, Duke, Beverly and their children would spend their first winter in the new house in Fallbrook, California, overlooking the sixty acres of avocado land Duke and Cliff owned.

It was a far cry from the tiny two-room trailer he and Beverly had occupied after their marriage in 1947. The fireplace in their large living room became the family pride and joy. Beverly called it "The Shrine." On the mantelpiece stood the glittering trophies Duke had collected over the last decade.

At this time Cliff and Duke decided to plant lemon and lime trees as well as avocados. They acquired a bulldozer and learned to manipulate it like a pair of experts. The partners put in long hours clearing, leveling and cultivating the earth. The regular early-to-bed early-to-rise farm routine kept Duke in top physical shape throughout the fall and winter.

When he could not resist the temptation of an occasional day off, he and Cliff headed out for a day of hunting rabbits, quail and ducks.

The home, the avocado ranch, the good health of his family, gave Duke a sense of genuine accomplishment as he faced the spring of 1957 and another baseball season.

At Vero Beach prior to spring training, Walter O'Malley announced his purchase of Wrigley Field in Los Angeles and the Angels' franchise in the Pacific Coast League at a cost of $3,250,000. This was O'Malley's last warning to the city of New York—build a new stadium or lose the Dodgers.

The fans screamed at this traitorous desertion by their gods; city officials made promises but did nothing. At spring training little else was discussed—Los Angeles would most certainly be the Dodgers' next home.

O'Malley's announcement disrupted team morale. For Gil Hodges, it would mean giving up a home. Gil lived in Brooklyn and was married to a Brooklyn girl. Campanella was worried that he would have to sell his business, probably at a loss.

In the clubhouse, the reporters turned to Snider. He lived in California and should be happy about the possibility of a move. Was he?

"Sure. It's home," Duke said. "That would be the good part. But I've spent ten seasons at Ebbets Field. I know what I can do and what I can't do in that ball park."

"Maybe if we win the World Series they'll give us Yankee Stadium and we won't have to go," Campy said.

Even another World Championship wouldn't have changed things, and the Dodgers were a long way from it in '57. Amazing things had happened to them in Brooklyn where people lived and died with their beloved "Bums." Brooklyn was less a place and more a state of mind. All this would be gone.

While the Dodgers were thinking about the Los Angeles move, Milwaukee took a commanding lead in the National League pennant race. After the All-Star break, Duke had gone on a tear, knocking out four homers in Brooklyn's next five winning games. It was a good try but in a lost cause. Milwaukee captured the flag, and Brooklyn came in third behind the Cardinals.

For the fifth straight season, Duke hit forty home runs or better. In '57 it was an even forty, just three under his all-time record of the previous year. But with his bad leg, his average had slipped to .274, the lowest in ten years.

On October 8, 1957, came the announcement all of Brooklyn had feared. Red Patterson, Walter O'Malley's public relations director, sounded the death knell. In fifty-one monumental words, he declared that the Dodgers would move to Los Angeles. The Los Angeles City Council had voted to take them with open arms. O'Malley was given 300 acres of Chavez Ravine on which to build a new stadium. In return, the wily club owner gave the city of Los Angeles Wrigley Field—all ten acres and 22,000 seats!

At least a decision had finally been reached. Duke could only hope it was for the best. Now, there was still one more decision, and this he would have to make alone. O'Malley wanted an operation performed on his star center fielder's knee.

"Duke," O'Malley asked, "how long do you want to play ball?"

"A few more years."

"Then have the operation. I've hired the best orthopedic surgeon in the country."

"I thought you said I had a choice."

"You do," O'Malley replied. "I just knew what it would be."

On December 18, 1957, Dr. Daniel Levinthal of Beverly Hills performed the delicate knee operation. While Duke was resting up, Cliff dropped by with the details of the agreement O'Malley had made with the city of Los Angeles.

"You mean we'll be playing in the Coliseum?" Duke asked with a pained expression.

Cliff nodded.

"But that's a football and track stadium, not a baseball park."

[151]

"It has one hundred and two thousand seats for the cash customers," Cliff replied.

Duke gazed at his bandaged knee. "I wish we were going back to Ebbets Field this spring," he said quietly. "That open-air monstrosity gives me the creeps."

Spring training for the Los Angeles Dodgers was still Vero Beach, Florida. With high hopes that his leg worries were over, Duke decided to drive down and was involved in a minor accident in Florida. The recently operated leg was hurt again and required treatment during most of spring training. That, in addition to the auto accident on Long Island which had tragically paralyzed Campanella and the retirement of Jackie Robinson, gave the Dodgers more than a few anxious moments as they looked ahead.

When the season opened, they lost the first game at the Coliseum to their arch rivals, the Giants, who had left New York and settled in San Francisco. The pain of that defeat was sweetened, however, by the turnout: 78,672 cash customers!

The mammoth stadium proved to be a gold mine for O'Malley and a monumental headache for his players. The moment Snider stepped through the players' gate on Menlo Street and took a good look at the right-field stands, he knew every game he played in the Coliseum would be sheer frustration. A solidly hit ball by a left-handed batter, a home run in any other ball park, would merely be a long out in the Coliseum.

On the other hand, left field began almost in back of

shortstop. When Carl Erskine saw it, he jokingly turned and started to walk out of the park. The only thing between a pitcher and every right-handed hitter who could drive a ball a mere 250 feet was a big screen.

"Look at that monster," Erskine said, referring to the screen. "We should never have left New York."

"Carl," Duke said with a sigh, "I've got a feeling you're absolutely right."

15

● ●

"Nineteen fifty-eight," one astute sportswriter noted, "will never be recalled fondly by Duke Snider as his year."

It started with the auto accident in Florida and ended with being hit on the head by a line drive.

Between times, Duke's biggest problem was keeping his temper in check. The bad knee had little to do with it. Trainer Doc Wendler had the leg more or less under control, but he couldn't control the comments from Dodger management, who kept placing the blame for the recurring injury on the ballplayer himself. This was one source of irritation; but a man could live with that. The real thorn in Duke's side was his powerfully hit drives that opposition fielders hauled down for easy outs in the football field the Dodgers now called home, the Los Angeles Coliseum.

Duke hated "the vast plain" separating right and center field fences from home plate. Each time he stepped to the plate, he glared angrily at his favorite home run zone in right center, which measured 440 backbreaking feet.

In his peak seasons from 1953 to 1957, Duke smashed 208 home runs, averaging 42 per season. In '58 he was to hit only 15!

And all around him right-handers were lobbing "powder-puff homers" over the short left-field Coliseum fence.

Duke's anger festered until he could scarcely keep it a secret.

"I used to break up a game," he complained to one reporter, "now I'm lucky to get on base. I'm just not a home run hitter in this park." The critical home run, the "game-breaker-up," had been his specialty. Now they were saying he had lost his grip.

Someone wanted to know if he had talked to O'Malley or Bavasi about it. "I'm just one of the hired help," Duke replied bitterly. "They won't change the stadium. I'll just have to change my style."

He began referring to the hated Coliseum as "the snake pit," and couldn't wait to get on the road. When the Giants played in Los Angeles, Willie Mays gazed at the right field fence and said: "Duke, I sure feel sorry for you."

No one felt sorrier for Duke than Duke himself, but there was nothing he could do about the situation. Then, one night during pregame practice, he finally exploded.

[155]

With a ball in his hand, he turned to Don Zimmer. "I'll get it out of this park one way or another!"

He took a hefty wind-up and let the ball fly toward the upper rim of the Coliseum. It didn't quite make it; the ball cleared only seventy-six of the seventy-nine rows of seats.

The enraged Duke grabbed another ball and tried again. This time he flung it as far as row seventy-eight. On the third try, he let out a cry of pain. The Coliseum had struck back. He had strained the muscle in his arm!

Sheepishly he wandered off to see Dr. Bob Woods, the club physician, who promptly declared: "That was a fool thing to do."

Duke could only nod. "I had to get it out of my system, Doc. This park is driving me nuts."

"Feel any better now?"

Duke shook his head. "I feel worse."

That night he had to be benched.

Buzzy Bavasi let out a roar that could be heard all the way back to Brooklyn. The Dodger general manager ordered Snider removed from the payroll until he was able to play again. "No play, no pay!"

Figured against Duke's $42,000 for the season, it meant he would lose $275 for every day he missed. Now it was his turn to roar.

"That's a slap in the face after all these years with the club!" he told one reporter, and then pointed out that Dodgers of former years had never been fined for "horseplay and fool pranks."

"When Dolph Camilli and Ernie Koy had a friendly

wrestling match in a Pullman car and Koy was out for a week with a wrenched knee," Duke recalled, "Durocher just wrote it off as a tough break."

The Associated Press headlined its story "Snider Lands in Dodgers' Doghouse," and it was carried in hundreds of papers across the country.

One enterprising sports writer in Los Angeles called Joe DiMaggio for a comment. Said Joe: "It was just a left-handed hitter feeling he had to get *something* out of that park."

After a night of heat treatments, the arm felt better, and he called on Manager Alston. "You can put me back in," he said.

"You sure?"

"I feel better. I'm sure!"

Alston put Duke back in the line-up, but he was a long way from being out of the doghouse.

The front-office grumbling continued. Snider didn't seem able to carry a full workload with his weakened knee. Alston began using him as a pinch hitter. Throughout the season, Duke would appear in only 106 games, and pinch-hit in 20 of these.

By late May, it was clear that both Duke and the Dodgers were jinxed. Duke's average dropped to .221 as the Dodgers languished in the cellar.

In the mind of Buzzy Bavasi, Snider and Dodger-trouble went hand-in-hand. Once again he used the press to lash out at Duke.

"As Snider goes," Bavasi fumed, "so go the Dodgers." And according to Bavasi, Duke wasn't going too well.

Duke had rarely been angrier. Why did they have to push? They knew his leg had to be drained periodically. That meant a day of treatment followed by a day of rest. It wasn't his idea. It was the doctor's orders.

"Give it up," he told himself. "Admit you're through." He shook away the thought. There had to be another way. Finally he decided to discuss it with his business partner.

"Cliff, there's one way to prove I've got something left as a ballplayer."

"Sure. Help them build the new ball park."

"Get some hits. Move the average up. And in the Coliseum that means changing my style. Not swinging so hard. Not uppercutting the ball to drive it out of the park. Just settling for a base hit dropped into right or right center field."

"You mean settle for ruining yourself! You know what Musial once said? 'The easiest way to kill a hitter is to mess with his natural swing.'"

"He's right. But what else can I do?"

Cliff had no answer.

The day Milwaukee came to the Coliseum decided Duke. He smashed a ball 425 feet to right center that Hank Aaron hauled in for an easy out. The second time up, Duke hit one to the exact same spot. This time Bill Bruton made the catch. The third time at bat, Duke tried to hit to left. He struck out.

That settled the question. He should ease up on his swing. Take the singles and stop slugging.

As it turned out, Duke had more flexibility than either

he or Cliff imagined. By the end of June his average had increased more than a hundred points! But the Dodgers still remained in the basement.

As for Duke, his good luck didn't last long. One day, while leading off third, he was smashed in the ear by a line drive. Duke never remembered hitting the ground. The smelling salts brought him around, but the doctor ordered X-rays. Though there appeared to be no major injury, Walter O'Malley was taking no chances. He ordered Duke sent home for the remaining weeks of the season. Neither Duke nor anyone else could help the seventh-place Dodgers. There was no sense risking further injury.

Duke worried as Beverly watched over him. It took three weeks for the dizziness to disappear. Throughout those anxious days, the thing he feared most was the possible loss of vision. He said nothing to Beverly. He just prayed.

The whole season had been a nightmare, the worst Duke had ever known. He lay in bed and looked out across the fields where the first avocado samplings were beginning to grow. In five years they would reach maturity and provide full harvests. In 1963 the avocados would give him economic independence. Could he last that long?

That winter Duke worked hard on the ranch. The knee responded well and did not have to be drained at all. He held his weight to a trim 195 pounds—ten below usual during the offseason.

[159]

He lived with full awareness that his playing days were numbered. Now, it was merely a question of how long he could put off the inevitable. The next five years seemed a big question mark.

Beverly understood her husband's worries, and one day happened to mention them to their friend Chuck Connors.

Chuck, star of the highly rated television series, "The Rifleman," decided he had exactly the right tonic for the disturbed ballplayer: a stint before the Hollywood TV cameras.

Next day, Connors was on the phone. "Duke, we're casting a villain who rides into North Fork, stirs up trouble and gets himself shot outside the town saloon."

"Great," Duke commented. "I'll watch it. When's it on."

"Next spring. First we have to shoot it. How about playing the part?"

"Me?" was the surprised reply.

"You!" said Connors.

Duke thought it was a gag. "You must be out of your mind. I can't act."

"You don't have to act," Connors said in all seriousness. "Just look mean."

Duke agreed to play the part of a Western villain, and thoroughly enjoyed the days spent at a Hollywood film studio.

When the show was aired, Gil Hodges promptly dispatched a wire to Duke: "Saw your last television show. Stop."

Duke laughed heartiest at the telegram received from Buzzy Bavasi: "You even favored your knee while you were falling dead."

By spring Duke felt good enough to volunteer for early training camp duty. It was the first time he had done that in thirteen major-league years.

The Dodger management had altered the right-field Coliseum fences to help left-handed sluggers, and hoped that Duke's eagerness was a sign of better things to come. They knew Snider had a great deal to protect: a $40,000 salary—he had been dropped $2,000 as a result of his poor year in '58—plus a reputation.

The way the front office figured, 1959 could be one of Duke's better years. If it was, the Dodgers might finally show the people of Los Angeles the stuff they were really made of.

16

●●●●●●●●●●●●●●●●●●●●●●●●●●●●●●●●●●●●●

To back up Snider and Furillo in the outfield for the '59 season, O'Malley had acquired Wally Moon from the Cardinals in a winter trade for Gino Cimoli. Most of the old-timers were gone: Newcombe, Campanella, Robinson, Reese. Duke had only Hodges and Furillo on the firing line with him from the great days in Brooklyn. Gil was still at first, with Charlie Neal at second, Bob Lillis and Don Zimmer rotating at shortstop, Jim Gilliam at third and Johnny Roseboro behind the plate.

The pitching staff consisted of Drysdale, Erskine, Labine, Sandy Koufax, Roger Craig, Don Bessent and Johnny Podres. On the bench sat such young hopefuls as outfielder Don Demeter, who would replace Duke if his knee acted up, catcher Norm Sherry and Norm's brother, rookie pitcher Larry Sherry.

It seemed to Duke a new generation of Dodgers had sprung up overnight, and he was determined to spark the newcomers to victory. The younger players began to look toward him for encouragement and leadership. If "broken-down Snider"—as he jokingly referred to himself—could deliver, so could they. Gilliam and Moon began to come through with the hits that counted. Still, no one seriously considered the Dodgers in contention for the 1959 pennant—except Duke Snider.

On April 24, with his knee taped as usual, Duke pinch-hit in a game against St. Louis that was tied 3–3 in the eleventh inning. Duke lined out a single, painfully beat it out to first driving in a run, and the Dodgers had the ball game 4–3.

On June 19 against the Reds, Duke won the game singlehandedly with two homers.

As O'Malley and Bavasi had so often said: "As Snider goes, so go the Dodgers."

Suddenly, the rest of the team seemed to catch fire. How far up from seventh place could the club climb?

The race, most experts felt, would be a knock-down drag-out fight between the Giants and the Braves. But by the end of June, the Dodgers had moved into second place on the heels of a seven-game winning streak as Gil Hodges started to drive the ball out of the park.

"If one old-timer can do it," Gil said with a nod toward Duke, "so can this one!"

Cautiously, Manager Alston mentioned possible pennant hopes. "We might win," he told a sports writer, "if Snider and Hodges keep on hitting."

Duke kept hitting. So did Hodges. And the Dodgers continued to make themselves felt among the first-division leaders.

On August 31, left-hander Sandy Koufax tied Bob Feller's modern major league strike-out record by fanning eighteen in a single game. The 5–2 win placed the Dodgers within one game of the league-leading Giants!

In the American League, the experts said, it was all over. The Chicago White Sox would soon have their first pennant in forty years. The Yankees were languishing in fourth place, sixteen and a half games off the pace.

On September 3 the Dodgers lost 5–3 to the Cards. That Sunday they dropped a double-header. According to the analysts the Dodgers had had it, they had been playing over their heads. Duke read the dire observations, grunted and cast them aside.

September 17, with nine games left in the season, found the Giants in first, Milwaukee in second and the Dodgers trailing by two games in third place.

"We need a miracle," one of the players commented in the clubhouse.

"What we need," Duke declared, "is a little relaxation." Secretly he had been waiting for just the right moment to extend the hospitality of the Snider home to his teammates. A party would snap the mounting tension. "You're all invited down to the ranch for a pig roast." The clubhouse rang with shouts of approval. "No excuses!"

Next day the Dodger caravan made its way 100 miles down the California coast to Duke's avocado ranch.

He provided a varied assortment of fun and sports: swimming, basketball, ping-pong, bridge, poker and horseshoes, but the center of attraction was a succulent forty-seven-pound roast pig, complete with apple in mouth. On one corner of the patio, Don Zimmer rendered a ragtime ukulele solo, while Junior Gilliam offered a golf demonstration on the lawn. In the kitchen Johnny Podres puffed on a cigar while he told a mournful tale of how he might be traded to the Yankees.

"I'm going to miss you guys," he said jokingly, "when I join the Yankees and wear a pin-stripe suit. That outfit is class!"

Manager Alston stepped up to the chow line as Duke dished out the food. "Thanks, Duke, we needed this," Alston said as he looked around at his relaxed, laughing ballplayers.

"This place was built with Dodger money," Duke replied sincerely. "It's the least I can do."

The next day would prove whether or not amateur psychologist Snider had called the turn as the Dodgers took on the Cincinnati Reds. Spirits stayed high; there was more talk about the roast pig than there was about baseball.

In the first inning Gilliam walked, Neal singled and then Duke stepped to the plate. He swung at a waist-high curve ball and the impact felt right. A towering 375-foot blast sailed over the right-field fence, Duke's twenty-second homer of the season.

That day the Dodgers moved into second place with a 4–3 victory. They won five of their next seven games, including a three-game weekend series from the Giants during which Duke hammered out his twenty-third homer. The Dodgers were now in first place by a half game!

Though the Giants had been overpowered, the Braves were still very much alive. On September 21, with Los Angeles idle, Milwaukee beat Pittsburgh to move into a first-place tie. There were now five games left in the season.

The following day, the Chicago White Sox clinched the American League crown. But in the National League no final decision was yet in sight. The Dodgers dropped a 11–10 heartbreaker to the Cardinals, while the Braves beat the Pirates, 5–3. Now Milwaukee was in first place.

On the twenty-third, the Dodgers won and the Braves lost. Again, the two teams were tied for first place. No games were scheduled for the twenty-fourth. On the twenty-fifth, the Phils beat Milwaukee while the Dodgers took the Cubs. The 5–4 Dodger victory came with an eleventh-inning home run by Gil Hodges.

But the sweet taste of league leadership was to linger for only a day. On the twenty-sixth, the Dodger-Brave seesaw swung the other way. The Dodgers lost, the Braves won, and now it was all tied up again.

The twenty-seventh of September was the last day of the season. The Dodgers won their game and so did the Braves. The fantastic late-season surge, inspired by the "old pros," had brought Los Angeles to a best-of-three playoff.

Duke had hung on to the bitter end, trying diathermy,

ultrasonic therapy, rubs, whirlpool baths. The only thing that seemed to ease the pain in his leg was injections of cortisone. The shots usually lasted about two weeks. Now the pain was back and Don Demeter took Duke's place in the outfield for the opening game of the playoffs. Manager Alston was confident. He wanted to save Duke for the Series. "Wonderful Walt," as he soon came to be called, turned out to have had the town's clearest crystal ball. The Dodgers took the first two games, 3–2 and 6–5, to bring California its first major league pennant in history. Never before had a team gone from seventh place the previous season to a league flag the next. They called the Dodgers "the greatest dark horse winner in baseball history."

On opening day in Chicago's Comiskey Park against the White Sox the Dodgers succumbed to the strain of the pennant battle and the playoff. They fell apart 10–0.

Nevertheless Walt Alston was pleased. "It's out of their system," he declared. "All the anxiety. Now they can play ball."

The Dodgers took game number two, 4–3, with Johnny Podres on the mound and Charlie Neal the hero with a two-run homer.

The Series moved back to Los Angeles, and again it was the "Old Guard" that came through. Before the largest Series crowd ever, 92,294 screaming California fans, Carl Furillo cracked out a pinch-hit bases-loaded single in the seventh to break open the ball game.

Next day, Hodges came through with an eighth-inning home run into the left-field seats. The Dodgers

[167]

took it, 5–4, while their vice president, Buzzy Bavasi, suffered a semicollapse from the excitement.

Los Angeles now led three games to two. Alston still kept Snider out of the line-up.

"How does it feel?" a reporter asked the inactive Duke after the Dodgers dropped game number five, 1–0.

Duke almost chopped the reporter's head off. "I don't like sitting on the bench. I hate it, but I know I can't help with my leg killing me. I can't hit and I can't cover ground. We carry enough extra outfielders. A Don Demeter at 100 per cent is a lot better than a Duke Snider at 50 per cent."

Duke moved away from the reporter and walked over to Walt Alston. They would be leaving for Chicago and would have a day's rest before game number six. "I'm ready to go back in," he told the Dodger manager.

"We're ready to have you back," Alston replied.

Game number six got under way in Chicago on October 8. It felt good to be back in center field. And in the third inning, with Wally Moon on base, Duke felt extra good as he stepped into a pitch and drove it over the right-field fence for his eleventh Series home run. In a thirteen-hit attack the Dodgers whipped the White Sox, 9–3, to give California its first World Series championship.

And standing beside Duke for the photographers' pictures was another Californian, a pitcher named Larry Sherry. Youth and age, side by side. Sherry, a strapping youngster from Los Angeles' Fairfax High School, had been recalled from the farm system in midseason. In the Series he had become the pitching sensation, figuring in all four Dodger victories. Sherry had won two and saved two, all in relief.

Sharing the spotlight with the rookie pitcher, suddenly Duke Snider felt very, very old.

17

On the night of August 26, 1960, more than 50,000 people gathered at the Coliseum to pay tribute to a native son.

It was "Duke Snider Night." The special ceremonies would come between games of a twi-night double-header against Cincinnati. Until then, Duke sat on the bench, waiting.

The Snider Night Committee, headed by Jack Lincoln, put on a dazzling salute. Duke walked out between Gil Hodges and Carl Erskine, and the fans gave him a standing ovation.

George Jessel, the master of ceremonies, waited for the applause to subside, then announced that the Sniders were expecting their fourth child. With that, he presented Duke with a baby's stay-put chair.

There followed an avalanche of gifts including an autographed silver platter from the entire Dodger team. Finally, Jack Lincoln stepped forward with the last gift.

Jack explained that in all World Series history, Duke Snider alone had hit four home runs in two different years. Yet, he had never received a World Series most valuable player award.

"Tonight," Lincoln declared, "we make up for the oversight." And with that he handed Duke the keys to a 1960 Corvette.

"I'll remember this night the rest of my life," Duke said. "I also can't forget another ball park which no longer stands, Ebbets Field in Brooklyn, and my performances there.

"I wish I could have been better out here." Duke wanted the hometown folks to know how he really felt. "I'll tell you one thing, it hasn't been from lack of trying."

The applause rang wild.

"Now everything would really be perfect if I could get a couple of good base hits."

If ever there was a time when Duke ached to come through, this was it. He stepped to the plate for the first time in the second inning. Facing him on the mound was Cincinnati hurler Cal McLish. Duke remembered back to 1944 when they had been together as Dodger rookies in spring training.

McLish pumped, delivered and Duke swung. At the crack of the bat, the fans rose to their feet, screaming. The roar built to a crescendo as the ball sailed a spectacular 410 feet over the center-field fence. The hero of the night romped around the bases as if on winged feet.

Who said he was old? Who said he didn't have it anymore? That ball over the fence was the 367th homer of his fourteen-year Dodger career, placing him just two behind the retired Ralph Kiner, who was seventh on the all-time home run roster.

In his second chance at bat that memorable night, Duke hit a triple giving him the club's all-time leadership in extra base hits, 767. The Dodgers won, 2–0, with Duke Snider enjoying one of the most glorious nights of his entire career.

In 1960 Duke played in 101 games, but his average slipped to .243. He hit only fourteen homers all season, and the Dodgers finished in fourth place.

The leg said quit, but Duke wasn't ready to give up. Not yet. He needed three more seasons before the avocados would take care of the Snider family.

Throughout the winter, Duke kept his weight down. He busied himself on the ranch and tried not to pay attention to the rumors that O'Malley might trade him to the Yankees. The oldest Dodger pro, they said, had had his day.

"O'Malley'll keep you," Cliff Dapper insisted. "You're a draw in Los Angeles. The Dodgers need every dollar they can get at the gate to pay for that stadium in Chavez Ravine."

Duke didn't argue. He would just wait and see, wait for a phone call. It came from Buzzy Bavasi as a New

Year's present. He was off the trading block. Negotiations with the Yankees, who had wanted Duke's left-hand hitting to take advantage of the Stadium fences as a pinch hitter, had been terminated formally and finally.

When the reporters called, Duke said he was pleased. "I'd rather be here. But I hope I get to play some more. I still have some pieces of unfinished business in this game of baseball." Duke meant the goal he had once set of 500 home runs as his lifetime ambition. He hoped to beat the all-time National League record of 511, set by Mel Ott, but the surgery on his knee coupled with the shift in ball parks made that impossible. Now, he could only hope to reach the 400 plateau. Duke also wanted to become a member of the exclusive 2,000-hit club. His current total stood at 1,892.

"The Dodgers have a fantastic future," Duke told one reporter. "I want to be part of it a few more years." To which he added: "A more active part than in 1960."

He reported to spring training in 1961 a trim 185 pounds, the lowest weight since his junior year in high school. Lean and hard, he looked forward to a good solid season.

Back in the regular line-up, he hammered out two homers in his first seven games, moving him ahead of Kiner's total. Now, he was in seventh place, behind Babe Ruth.

Then came Duke's next trip to the plate in a game against the Cardinals. Bob Gibson's first pitch was wide; the next one came inside fast and hard. It caught Duke on the elbow with a vicious crack that sent an agonizing pain through his body. As he slumped to his knees, he knew his arm was broken.

The next month was sheer frustration as Duke sat on the sidelines wearing a cast. In July, though the fracture had healed and the cast was removed, he found himself still warming the bench.

"I'm not helping the club by just sitting here," he told a sports writer. "I want to go where I can play."

The idleness irritated him, and like any good hitter, unless he was permitted to bat steadily, his timing dropped off.

The continued frustration erupted in anger the day an umpire accused Duke of shouting at him from the bench.

"You've got the wrong guy!" the outraged Snider insisted, but the umpire fined him fifty dollars.

Finally, in mid-July, Duke returned to action. In a three-week period, he snagged thirteen hits in forty-one times at bat for a .328 average with four homers and twelve runs batted in. He topped it off with three hits in a 7–3 victory over Milwaukee, including a homer, which stretched the Dodger's league lead to four games over the Reds.

But by season's end, the positions were reversed. The Reds went to play the Yankees in the World Series, leaving the bewildered Dodgers at home in second place. A ten-game losing streak late in August had spelled doom to the Dodger pennant hopes. Playing in only eighty-five games, Duke finished with .296, more than fifty points above his 1960 average.

Again that winter there was trade talk involving Duke Snider. Nothing came of it, and at the end of February he was appointed Dodger field captain, the first since Pee Wee Reese in 1958.

A beaming, handsome man of thirty-five with steel-gray hair, Duke made one of the shortest acceptance speeches in baseball history. "The only thing I can say is let's win."

But for Duke, 1962 was a carbon copy of the previous season. He played in only eighty games, hit just five home runs, and dropped almost twenty points in his average. He was in the starting line-up only thirty-seven times, and for one stretch of eleven weeks he did nothing but pinch-hit.

For the second year in a row, the Dodgers were favored to win the pennant, but as Arthur Daley of *The New York Times* put it, "a funny thing happened to the Dodgers on their way to the World Series." They frittered away a championship they had already won, by allowing the Giants to tie them for the flag on the last day of the season. A comfortable lead disappeared, and they were forced into a three-game playoff battle.

Duke was sidelined during the first game, and San Francisco won it, 8–0. In game number two, Alston decided to bring Duke in. He played left field, got one hit, and the Dodgers took it, 8–7. In the final game, Duke came through with two hits, but the Giants made history repeat itself. Eleven years before, they had brought the Dodgers down in the ninth inning of the deciding play-off game on the wings of Bobby Thomson's electrifying three-run homer. Now, in a ninth-inning rally, they did it again to win, 6–4. For Duke the whole season had been a keen disappointment. His career had come to a dead stop. He wasn't doing himself or the Dodgers much good.

"I'm ready to be traded," Duke finally announced to the team's general manager.

Buzzy Bavasi stared hard at the star outfielder who had labored for sixteen long years in behalf of the Dodger organization. He knew Duke as a man who couldn't be tied to a bench, a man who had to be in action.

Bavasi thought a moment, said nothing, then nodded and walked off.

18

●●●●●●●●●●●●●●●●●●●●●●●●●●●●●●●●●●●●●●●

After an exhibition game between the Dodgers and Yanks on March 14, 1963, at Fort Lauderdale, Buzzy Bavasi announced the Dodger plans for Duke Snider.

"The Mets get the first shot at him. I'd like to see Duke go to New York. I'm a National League man and I'm thinking of the league. He'd be worth 300,000 in attendance."

Met president and ex-Yankee general manager George Weiss admitted interest in adding the name of Duke Snider to the roster of his year-old team. Casey Stengel, whom Weiss had brought out of retirement at the age of seventy-one to manage the New York team, could scarcely curb his enthusiasm. "I'd give O'Malley a million dollars for him!"

All that remained to complete the deal was Weiss' agreement to spend $78,000—$38,000 in salary to Duke plus $40,000 more to the Dodgers. Clearly, this would be one of baseball's biggest bargains.

On April 1 Duke Snider became a Met.

Duke heard about it in Albuquerque where the Dodgers were playing an exhibition game. His teammates gathered around, trying to keep it bright and gay, but emotion got the better of them all. Before the good-byes were over, Duke broke down and wept unashamedly. Through his tears he looked at Don Drysdale and grinned. "You big lug, you just try to strike me out. I'll be knocking those pitches of yours right over the fence."

Before boarding the plane for a quick visit with his family, Duke stopped off to see the team's venerable equipment manager, John Griffin. He handed back to Griffin a uniform with the number four he had given Duke many years ago.

Duke said simply, "Thanks."

Griffin understood. He had seen Dodger players come and go since 1917. The old man gazed thoughtfully at the uniform Duke had made famous.

"Remember when I told you Dolph Camilli wore that number and to do it justice?"

Duke nodded. "A long time ago."

Griffin began to fold the uniform carefully, as if it were something special, something precious. Finally, he looked up.

"I'm asking Mr. O'Malley to retire the number in

your honor—just like the Yankees did for Babe Ruth, Lou Gehrig and Joe DiMaggio."

"Duke of Dodgerdom Still King" was the apt description by *The Sporting News* of opening day 1963. More than 25,000 fans crowded into the ancient Polo Grounds to give Duke Snider a standing ovation. Among the Met teammates on hand to greet him were six former Dodgers: Tim Harkness, Larry Burright, Roger Craig, Norm Sherry, Charlie Neal and his close friend Gil Hodges.

Duke Snider Fan Clubs showed themselves everywhere in the stands. Whistles blew and horns screeched. Flags and banners hung from the bleachers. "Your Loyal Fans!" "Welcome Back Duke" and "It's Worth the Loot for Duke," they read.

It was good to be back in New York, to be wanted and accepted, Duke thought. It was good to have a new start with a young team. "Like being born again."

Though the Mets didn't win often, there was hope and promise—New Yorkers had missed that for too long. With the Dodgers and the Giants in California, there were only the Yankees. And the Yankees didn't need moral support. For them, winning was almost a foregone conclusion. That left the citizens of the great metropolis with no one to root for. New Yorkers love an underdog, and in the Mets they found that hint of tomorrow's greatness.

The Mets had lost a record 120 games during 1962, their first season. But to the fans that proved just one thing: the only place they could go was up.

In Cincinnati on April 16, Duke collected hit number 2,000 in the second inning of a game against the Reds. Then, on June 14, again against Cincinnati, Duke finished the last of his "unfinished business."

With two out in the first inning and a man on base, he slammed the ball 375 feet into the right-field seats. It was the milestone for which he had waited so long: the 400th homer of his career! And it came with a 10–3 Met victory.

That four-bagger made Duke the ninth player in baseball history to achieve 400 home runs.

On August 8, Duke received the New York Catholic Youth Organization Award from the Reverend John N. Brooks, who praised him for the excellent example of sportsmanship he had set for the youth of New York and the nation.

After the award ceremony, a reporter asked Duke about the 1964 season.

"I have to think about it," he said. "I probably won't decide until the winter." Duke thought of his average and how hard it had been to get it above the present .250 level. He wondered again, should he quit? He didn't just want to hang on. He had the avocados now and no longer had to depend on baseball for his income. Stengel would certainly keep him as a pinch hitter, under any circumstances. But did he want that?

Duke moved past the reporter and headed for the locker room, where he wrapped a heat pad around his aching knee. Gazing at the leg that had plagued him so long, he wondered if it could stand the strain of still-another season. He hated to be forced to give up.

On September 12, Duke became the last player to be honored at the soon-to-be-demolished Polo Grounds. In '64, the Mets would be playing in brand new Shea Stadium in the Flushing Meadow section of New York City.

Before the Mets faced pitcher Juan Marichal and the Giants on September 12, Duke stood at home plate while sports announcer Lindsey Nelson called out those teammates of old who had come to pay tribute on "Duke Snider Night": Hall-of-Famer Jackie Robinson; twenty-seven-game winner Don Newcombe; Cookie Lavagetto, now a Met coach; Gil Hodges, who had become manager of the Washington Senators; Ralph Branca, who had pitched his way to fame at age twenty-one by winning twenty-one games; great outfielder Carl Furillo; and pitcher Carl Erskine. A great cheer went up as the indomitable Roy Campanella was wheeled out to shake Duke's hand and say: "Good to be with you."

Though it was a night for Duke as a Met in the Polo Grounds, to him it was really a night in Brooklyn with Roy and Gil and Jackie and Carl. Memories of another day. Introduced as "the last of the great ones from Ebbets Field," Duke stepped to the mike and waited for the applause to subside.

"I want to tell all my friends one thing—you can't take the Dodgers out of Brooklyn."

The fans roared. They loved Duke for it. This might be a big night in the Polo Grounds but Duke and the fans knew it belonged in Ebbets Field.

"Let's get the game going," he finally said. "I'm too nervous."

Duke walked, grounded out and struck out twice in four trips to the plate as the Giants beat the Mets, 6–0. Each time he came to bat, the fans applauded loudly, urging him on. Duke wished he could have done better that night, but it was still a joy just to be there and try. He had told himself he would retire at the end of 1963, but he changed his mind when the venerable Casey came over to shake his hand.

"Duke," Casey said, "I've seen them all, and in my book you'll always belong right up there with the very best—playing, coaching or managing."

Coaching or managing? Duke hadn't really thought much about staying in baseball after his playing days were over. But why not? Sixteen years in the majors had taught him plenty he could pass along to younger men. What if he did have a few gray hairs? He'd get his weight down under 200 pounds during the winter, then go for another season at brand new Shea Stadium, playing and maybe coaching, too.

"Thanks," Duke smiled as he pumped Casey's hand. "What for?"

"Giving me something to think about this winter."

Duke finished the '63 season with a .243 average. It didn't look like much, but he had played in forty-nine more games than the previous year and almost doubled his number of hits.

As he headed back to California that fall to family

and friends, Duke was filled with renewed vigor and an abiding sense of satisfaction. He had achieved the goals set in his schoolboy days.

In January 1964 he signed a contract to play another year with the Mets. His career wasn't over. In some way it might only be just beginning.

EDWIN DONALD (DUKE) SNIDER
Born, September 19, 1926   Height—6'   Weight—195
Bats left and throws right

Year	Club	League	G	AB	R	H	2B	3B	HR	RBI	SB	Avg.
1944	Montreal	Int.	2	2	0	0	0	0	0	0	0	.000
1944	Newport News	Piedmont	131	507	87	149	34*	6	9*	50	10	.294
1945						(In the U.S. Navy)						
1946	Ft. Worth	Texas	68	232	36	58	13	1	5	30	5	.250
1947	St. Paul	A.A.	66	269	59	85	22	7	12	46	4	.316
1947	Brooklyn	N.L.	40	83	6	20	3	1	0	5	2	.241
1948	Montreal	Int.	77	275	67	90	28	4	17	44	8	.327
1948	Brooklyn	N.L.	53	160	22	39	6	6	5	21	4	.244
1949	Brooklyn	N.L.	146	552	100	161	28	7	23	92	12	.292
1950	Brooklyn	N.L.	152	620	109	199*	31	10	31	107	16	.321
1951	Brooklyn	N.L.	150	606	96	168	26	6	29	101	14	.277
1952	Brooklyn	N.L.	144	534	80	162	25	7	21	92	7	.303
1953	Brooklyn	N.L.	153	590	132*	198	38	4	42	126	16	.336
1954	Brooklyn	N.L.	149	584	120†	199	39	10	40	130	6	.341
1955	Brooklyn	N.L.	148	538	126*	166	34	6	42	136*	9	.309
1956	Brooklyn	N.L.	151	542	112	158	33	2	43*	101	3	.292
1957	Brooklyn	N.L.	139	508	91	139	25	7	40	92	3	.274
1958	Los Angeles	N.L.	106	327	45	102	12	3	15	58	2	.312
1959	Los Angeles	N.L.	126	370	59	114	11	2	23	88	1	.308
1960	Los Angeles	N.L.	101	235	38	57	13	5	14	36	1	.243
1961	Los Angeles	N.L.	85	233	35	69	8	3	16	56	1	.296
1962	Los Angeles	N.L.	80	158	28	44	11	3	5	30	2	.278
1963	New York	N.L.	129	354	44	86	8	3	14	45	0	.243
Major League Totals			2,052	6,994	1,243	2,081	351	85	403	1,316	99	.298

* Led league
† Tied for league lead

EDWIN DONALD (DUKE) SNIDER
WORLD SERIES RECORD

Year	Club	League	G	AB	R	H	2B	3B	HR	RBI	Avg.
1949	Brooklyn	N.L.	5	21	2	3	1	0	0	0	.143
1952	Brooklyn	N.L.	7	29	5	10	2	0	4	8	.345
1953	Brooklyn	N.L.	6	25	3	8	3	0	1	5	.320
1955	Brooklyn	N.L.	7	25	5	8	1	0	4	7	.320
1956	Brooklyn	N.L.	7	23	5	7	1	0	1	4	.304
1959	Los Angeles	N.L.	4	10	1	2	0	0	1	2	.200
World Series Totals			36	133	21	38	8	0	11	26	.286

Index

●●●●●●●●●●●●●●●●●●●●●●●●●●●●●●●●●●●●●

About the Author

IRWIN WINEHOUSE has been a free-lance writer throughout most of his adult life. At the age of nineteen he sold his first story, a radio script, to CBS, then began writing for the men's adventure magazines, finally becoming a featured columnist for *Saga*. Then followed a seven-year stint in Hollywood writing more than fifty TV and motion picture scripts. His latest screen story is being filmed on location in Greece. Born in the Bronx, home of the New York Yankees, Mr. Winehouse confesses to becoming a Brooklyn fan during the '40s. A graduate of DeWitt Clinton High School and New York University, he now lives in Silvermine, Connecticut.